The Wisdom
of the Runes

Odin by Ólafur Brynjúlfssons, from *Edda*, 1760. (Reproduced by permission of University College Library, London.)

The
Wisdom of the
RUNES

Michael Howard

RIDER
London Melbourne Sydney Auckland Johannesburg

Readers who are seriously interested in the practical application of the Norse and Saxon versions of the pagan Old Religion in contemporary society are invited to contact the author for further information

Rider & Company

An imprint of the Hutchinson Publishing Group

17–21 Conway Street, London W1P 6J D

Hutchinson Publishing Group (Australia) Pty Ltd
16–22 Church Street, Hawthorn, Melbourne, Victoria 3122

Hutchinson Group (N Z) Ltd
32–34 View Road, P O Box 40–086, Glenfield, Auckland 10

Hutchinson Group (S A) Pty Ltd
P O Box 337, Bergvlei 2012, South Africa

First published 1985
© Michael Howard 1985

Set in 10/11$\frac{1}{2}$ Plantin

Printed and bound in Great Britain by Anchor Brendon Ltd, Tiptree, Essex

ISBN 0 09 159911 3

This book is humbly dedicated to all true seekers of the Ancient Wisdom. May their chosen path be illuminated by knowledge, understanding and the inner light of spiritual revelation

Contents

A great value of antiquity lies in the fact
that its writings are the only ones that
modern men still read with exactness.

Nietzsche (1844–1900)

Part One

THE ORIGINS OF THE RUNES

1

During the last twenty years in the West there has been a growing interest in various forms of oriental religion such as Buddhism, Hinduism and Taoism. This interest has manifested itself on the popular level in such activities as yoga, transcendental meditation and the widespread establishment of Eastern religious cults centred on self-styled gurus. As an opposite reaction to this influx of Eastern religions there has also been an increased interest shown by many people seeking spiritual truths in the ancient Celtic cultures and their esoteric philosophies. This has led to the revival of Celtic art as a spiritual force, the formation of neo-Druidic study groups and the creation of pagan circles claiming traditional links with the Celtic version of the pre-Christian Old Religion.

Only recently, within the last eight or nine years, has there been any sign of a revival of interest in the non-Celtic forms of the ancient religious beliefs practised by the Anglo-Saxons and the Scandinavians. In the last few years serious research has been expanding in this field and especially in relation to the Saxon and Nordic Runes. Initially this research was of a superficial nature dealing in an elementary way with the runic alphabet as a system of divination. Although this is an important aspect of the Runes they also have a spiritual significance associated with the Northern European pagan religion which originated in the Neolithic and Bronze Ages.

The purpose of this book is threefold: first, to explore the Runes from a historical perspective and trace their origins; second, to reveal their practical use as a powerful method of predicting the future; third, to consider them as archetypal symbols representing a spiritual belief system comparable to such oriental philosophies as the I Ching and the Tao. With the present disillusionment with established religion it is only to be expected that intelligent people will seek alternative forms of spirituality. In presenting the ancient wisdom of the Runes the purpose is to show those seeking a new spiritual reality that a Western-based philosophy exists to which they can easily relate because its major symbols are etched deep into our national folk consciousness.

Even the names of the days of the week are derived from the old Norse gods and goddesses. Their titles are further recorded in many popular British placenames which are relics from the days of Viking and Saxon domination.

When these ancient archetypal symbols are invoked the results can be quite dramatic. As the Scottish writer Fiona MacLeod put it so clearly, 'The Old Gods are not dead – we are.' Beneath the surface of modern society the pagan gods still weave their spells of enchantment. Critics of the pagan spiritual belief system frequently condemn it as atavistic, primitive or barbaric. Certainly there are aspects of the old paganism which are not easy for modern people to understand and relate to. There will be no attempt in this book to gloss over the darker aspects of the worship of the pagan gods. They have to be recognized and accepted within their historical framework, just as we have to accept the darker side of our contemporary world. However, a serious and unbiased study of paganism, and especially its relationship with the new ecological insights being offered today, will reveal that it is relevant to our present planetary crisis. As humankind struggles against all odds to prevent its own and nature's destruction, the teachings of the pagan Old Religion offer us a way forward. These teachings are revealed through the use of the Runes, which offer a pagan blueprint for both personal and collective spiritual enlightenment.

Obviously any mention of the word 'rune' today conjures up bizarre images of secret magical incantations, curses and the dark sorcery of the Middle Ages. Casting the Runes has become in popular folklore something related to black magic, horror movies and the fantasies of supernatural thriller writers. In fact the Runes, in either their Norse or Saxon versions, have nothing to do with weird rites held under a gibbous moon or any of the other nightmares of the pseudo-occult world. The Runes are a magical and sacred alphabet used by the ancient peoples of Northern Europe for both secular and spiritual purposes, including divining the future. Their unwarranted sinister image arose as a result of the rejection of the pagan wisdom by the medieval Christian Church. With the coming of Christianity the Old Ways were outlawed as devil worship and black magic. The pagan practices which were prohibited included various occult (hidden) methods for predicting the future, for the Christian priests believed only God could have knowledge of such matters. The pagans were by Christian definition 'godless' and must therefore be deluded by the devils they worshipped as gods when they claimed to be able to foretell future events. The term 'pagan' is derived from the Latin *paganus*, meaning a person who dwells in the country. It is a reference to a period when the educated townspeople of the Roman Empire were being converted to the new religion while the country folk still followed the Old Ways.

Although by the Middle Ages the word 'rune' had degenerated to such an extent that it was commonly used to describe any magical word or symbol used in a spell or incantation, its original meaning reflected the Ancient Wisdom tradition it really represented. The word 'rune' can be traced back to the Old Norse *run*, which means a mystery or a secret. Hence in the epic Anglo-Saxon poem *Beowulf* the privy counsellor of royalty is called a 'Run-Wita' or a wise person who knows secrets. *Run* possibly came from the Old German *runa*, meaning 'a whisperer', and originally from the Indo-European root word *ru*, meaning 'a mysterious secret thing'. The old-fashioned slang phrase 'to rown', 'roon' or 'round' in the ear of another person was in common use in Anglo-Saxon and early medieval times. It indicated the passing on of secret information or gossip in a whisper.

It is evident that the secret information thus imparted may not have always been the latest petty gossip of court or village. The indication that the secrets whispered were in some way a mystery suggests an oral method of teaching arcane knowledge. In the classical world of Rome and Greece the specific term 'mystery religion' was used exclusively for forms of spirituality involving the initiation of the seeker into a secret cult which promised direct contact with the gods or divine forces symbolically representing the different aspects of nature. These mystery cults flourished underground as alternatives to the state religion, or existed as a secret teaching reserved for a small group of the established priesthood.

Therefore it can be safely assumed that the Runes, while used as a secular alphabet, originally had a deep spiritual meaning. The person who whispered secrets or the Runes was either a priest or priestess of the pagan Old Religion or a shaman (magician) operating outside the official priesthood. Some etymologists have suggested that the term *runa* denotes not only a whisperer of secrets but 'one who knows', i.e. a 'Wise One' who practices the secret arts of magic. When magic is referred to in the context of this book it is not the fairground tricks of the conjurer but a complex system of psycho-spiritual exercises designed to create changes in the consciousness of the magician. The people who used the Runes for magical purposes believed that the life force which resides in all living things and in many inanimate objects can be used to produce subtle changes in reality. Many of these effects are of a psychological nature, but that does not diminish their impact in either an ancient or a modern setting.

As an interesting sidelight on the *runa* or person who whispers secrets being a magician, a parallel can be drawn between this definition and the ancient cult of the Horse Whisperers. This was a rural secret society organized on Masonic lines which recruited its members from the ranks of stable lads, blacksmiths and farm labourers who worked with horses. Members of the fraternity allegedly possessed some secret knowledge or magical power enabling them to calm wild horses and heal sick animals. These acts were accomplished by the use of spells, incantations and the whispering of secret formulas into the ears of horses. These formulas were a closely guarded secret within the Horse Whisperers. They were passed on to new initiates only after the latter had taken a bloodcurdling oath of allegiance to the other members. Blacksmiths were often elected as Grand Masters of the fraternity because traditionally they have always been regarded by country people as natural magicians. Possibly the Horse Whisperers may be a surviving relic of the ancient pre-Christian worship of horses as sacred animals of the gods. Horse worship was widespread in the Iron Age among the Celts, Scandinavians and Germans. It is believed that the Society of Horse Whisperers or Horsemen's Word still exists in remote country areas, especially in Scotland and East Anglia.

Where and when did the Runes as an alphabet originate? The origin of the Runes is perhaps the most incomprehensible mystery of all. More nonsense has been written about this subject than about all forms of ancient alphabets, including both the Hebrew and Egyptian, which have also been credited with magical and religious significance.

Some experts in the origins of ancient languages and alphabets have surmised that the Runes are derivatives of the standard Latin alphabet and are therefore of relatively recent genesis. This theory takes as its starting point the undisputed fact that several of the runic characters are similar to letters of the Latin alphabet. One German expert has dated the Runes to the early Christian period, while another claims that the alphabet developed in the period when the Roman armies occupied Germany. It was then carried northwards by travellers to Scandinavia. Yet another expert alleges that the Runes are of Greek origin and were adopted by the Goths from a mixture of the Greek and Roman alphabets. According to this theory, the Runes originated in the Black Sea area around the third century of the common era. They were then carried home by German mercenaries and eventually reached the Nordic regions.

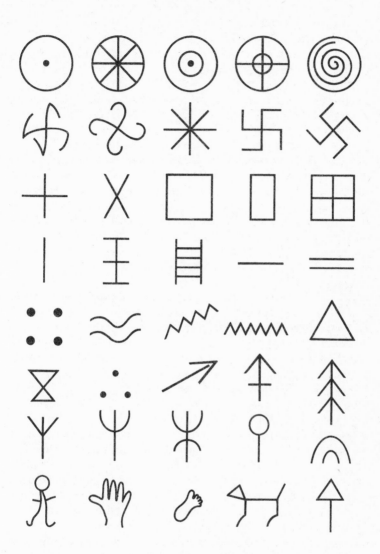

THE HALLRISTINGER SCRIPT

This ancient script which survives in rock carvings is one of the oldest forms of European writing. Each symbol has a special significance in the shamanistic religious tradition and includes symbols of solar worship, fertility, the stars and the Cosmos and mystical concepts. The Hallristinger script is believed to be the forerunner of the runic alphabet which it closely resembles

According to Professor R.W. Elliott, there are many criticisms of the Greek and Latin theories. He believes the Runes may have developed in the North Italian Alpine region and, while they have obvious similiarities with the orthodox Latin alphabet, they are of a very ancient lineage. To justify his statement Elliott cites the use of magical symbols or letters carved on sticks as a form of divination by the ancient tribes who inhabited the Italian Tyrol. This practice is very similiar to the carving of Runes on special pieces of wood used to divine the future by both the German and Norse priesthood.

Elliott further speculates that some early Rune Master from Germany was introduced to the Runes in their Italian form and adopted them for his personal use. From Germany they would have passed north along the established trade routes to the coastal tribes living by the North Sea. Thence they would have entered Jutland and Scandinavia. Although the Runes have similarities with the Latin alphabet and can be translated directly into the English letters of our modern one, it seems likely they have a separate origin in prehistory.

Experts have pointed out that the Runes may possibly possess a common ancestry with the prehistoric rock carvings known as the Hallristinger script used by the Neolithic and Bronze Age peoples. It has been suggested that the sharp angular strokes of the Runes are due to the fact that originally they were carved in stone. Such a method of recording an ancient script or alphabet would preclude the use of rounded or curved letters.

The Hallristinger script was used primarily by the Bronze Age people who lived *circa* 1300–1200 BCE. The script, like the ancient Egyptian hieroglyphics, consists of symbols which have a religious meaning. They include several variations on the circle: a circle with a dot in the centre, circles with equal-armed crosses inside them, and smaller circles with eight rays extending from the centre. All these represent the sun and suggest pagan solar worship. Other Hallristinger script sigils such as spirals, wavy lines and inverted triangles can be identified as magico-religious symbols associated with female sexuality and the worship of the Great Mother Goddess.

Prominent in the Hallristinger script is the swastika. This ancient sign has been debased by its use during the period 1933–45 by the German National Socialist Party. They adopted the swastika as their emblem because of its magical significance and its use by the old Indo-European or Aryan culture. In doing so, they destroyed its previous widespread symbolism as a representation of the life force. Many of the leading National Socialists, including Adolf Hitler, were interested in the Runes. They were therefore well aware of the swastika's ancient relationship to the religious ideas which formed the spiritual foundation of the runic system.

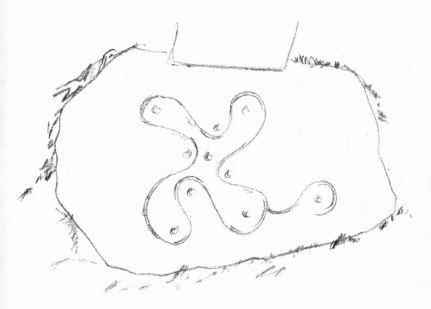

'Swastika Stone', Ilkley Moor

The swastika has very ancient origins. A rock carving dating from the prehistoric period near Ilkley in Yorkshire displays a swastika symbol. Another swastika is to be found on a piece of medieval graffiti in a church at Sutton in Bedfordshire. A drawing shows a dancing male figure with long flowing hair. One hand is upraised while the other points downwards in a classic ritual gesture indicating that heaven and earth are one. On the chest of the dancing figure is the representation of a stylized swastika. This particular design is identical to others found in the church of Little Waltham in Essex, in the Hallristinger script and on the prehistoric stone in Yorkshire.

The swastika is a universal archetypal symbol. In various forms it is to be found in Aztec, Buddhist, Chinese, Finnish, Hindu, native American, Saxon and Norse religions. The word *swastika* is Sanscrit

and means literally 'all is well'. It is believed to derive from the sun
wheel or equal-armed cross within a circle, which is another important
Hallristinger script symbol. It denotes the daily movement of the sun
across the sky and the annual cycle of the seasons, which were recorded
ritually in pagan religious observance. In the Far East the swastika is
universally recognized as a symbol of good health, happiness, good
fortune and cosmic perfection.

Although the German National Socialist Party may have specifically
adopted the swastika as their political badge because it was a pagan
symbol, there is evidence that it was used by the Church during the
medieval period. Nigel Pennick, who has written extensively on both
the swastika and the Runes, has claimed that the mitre worn by
Thomas Beckett when he was murdered had a border of swastikas. It
also had the pagan inscription 'Hail to thee O Earth Mother of Man.
May ye thrive in God's embrace. Overflow with fruit for man's ben-
efit.' It has been rumoured that Beckett had clandestine links with
either the pagan Old Religion or the heretical Cathar religion and that
his death was a ritual murder. Pennick also cites the Christian use of
the swastika in a stained-glass window of the Holy Sepulchre church in
Cambridge, and in a church at Cliffory, County Sligo, where a stone of
unknown age is carved with both a Celtic cross and a swastika. All
these Christian examples may be pagan survivals, but what are we to
make of a carved swastika found in the ruins of an ancient Jewish
synagogue in East Jordan and mentioned by Pennick?

The swastika has direct links with the Runes through the
Hallristinger script and also by the fact that it is often found in the
vicinity of runic symbols. One classic example is the famous standing
stone at Hogby in Sweden. This stone has several Runes carved on it as
well as equal-armed crosses, Christian Calvary crosses, spirals and
swastikas. Pennick cites the Scandinavian influence on nearby
Finland, which also has its native shamanistic traditions. As late as
1939 aeroplanes of the Finnish Air Force carried the swastika insignia
on their wings. Both military and civilian medals issued by the Finnish
government employed the swastika in their design. As soon as German
troops invaded France in 1940 the swastika vanished from sight except
on National Socialist flags and military insignia. Earlier in the 1930s
the English writer Rudyard Kipling ordered that the swastika which
had previously adorned the covers of his books should be removed.
Kipling was no advocate of National Socialism but, as a passionate
lover of India, had used the swastika in its ancient sense as a good-luck
charm.

The National Socialists adopted the swastika because it was a mystical symbol which had considerable significance to the Aryan or Indo-European race. According to their political ideology, an Aryan was any non-Jewish person of Teutonic or Nordic stock. The word *aryan* is Sanscrit for 'noble' and refers to the horse-riding warrior peoples who emerged near the Caspian Sea with a separate racial identity around 3000 BCE. They were the ancestors of the German, Roman, Greek, Slavic and Iranian tribal peoples who formed the foundation of the present European family of racial types. The Aryans or Indo-Europeans tamed wild horses, reared cattle and worshipped gods and goddesses who were personifications of the forces of nature. These Aryan people invaded India around 1500 BCE and colonized ancient Greece and Asia Minor.

Hitler fervently believed that the German race was descended from this ancient race of noble warriors. At the height of the last war he dispatched expeditions to India and Tibet seeking evidence to support his racial theories. Specifically, these expeditions were hoping to make contact with a semi-legendary tribe of white Aryans supposed to be living in a remote valley in the Himalayas. This mysterious tribe may have been the original model for the Hidden Masters or the Great White Brotherhood which nineteenth-century theosophical occultists believed lived in Tibet and guided the affairs of humanity. Although Hitler's expeditions failed, in 1984 it was revealed that a French explorer had made contact with these people, but until he publishes his findings it is difficult to know if their existence proves the National Socialist theories of German racial purity. It seems very unlikely.

Ignoring Hitler's racial fantasies, we can historically trace the origin of the Germanic and Scandinavian races who used the Runes. The first detailed references to the Germanic tribes were made by Julius Caesar, who campaigned against the Celts in Gaul and Britain. Caesar encountered the Germani, who lived in Scandinavia and what is now the northern part of Germany. It seems that the Germani were closely related to the Celts and shared a common Indo-European ancestry. In fact, in the second century BCE the Germani and Celtic tribes united to attack the armies of the Roman Empire.

Although the civilized Romans regarded all other races as barbarians (from the Greek *barbaros*, meaning 'foreigner' but now used to denote a wild or uncultured person), the Germani people had a very complex and, by contemporary standards, sophisticated social structure. They lived in well-built villages and on large farms where they raised cattle and grew crops. Their houses were strongly built with wattle walls, clay floors and thatched roofs supported by crossbeams. Next to the dwelling houses in the villages were smaller buildings, identified by archaeologists as workshops, bakeries, food stores, weaving sheds and barns.

Although the Germani and the Romans were enemies during various historical periods, they also had extensive trade links, dealing in gold and silver, jewellery, pottery and weapons. This exchange of trade was on both sides, with the Romans purchasing as many products from the so-called barbarians as the latter did from Rome. Even after the collapse of the Roman Empire these important trading links survived as Germani merchants dealt with the Near East and the Byzantine empire.

A considerable amount of our knowledge of the Germanic tribes comes from Cornelius Tacitus. He was a Roman soldier, senator and historian who died in 120 CE. In his famous book *Germania* he describes the customs and social relationships of the German tribes. He had a poor opinion of the degenerate Roman society of his time and frequently contrasted the debased activities of his countrymen with the virtues of German tribal society. Certainly there is little evidence that Tacitus subscribed to the widely held belief among his contemporaries that the barbarian world began outside the gates of Roman cities.

As an ex-soldier Tacitus was naturally interested in the fighting skills of the German tribes and in their weaponry. He describes how they used short spears with narrow blades which could be used either at close range or thrown like a javelin. Often the soldiers fought naked (Celtic-fashion) or clad in short woollen cloaks. From other sources we know that the Germans favoured barbed javelins, double-bladed throwing axes and the seax, which was a short broadsword of Roman style. Shields seem to have been used both as a defence and symbolically. Any warrior who threw away his shield during a battle was dishonoured and forbidden to attend religious rites.

Socially, Tacitus tells us, the Germani chose their rulers because they were men and women of noble birth. The spiritual tradition of divine kingship was well established among the peoples of tribal Europe. Their army commanders relied on example rather than authority, often leading their men into battle. Tacitus also records that the Germani carried religious emblems, totems and divine images from their sacred groves into battle to protect their troops from the enemy. They often dedicated themselves to the war god Tyr before marching into battle. The soldiers were also accompanied by their families on campaigns away from home. The Romans reported that

Germani armies on the brink of defeat were rallied by the sight of their womenfolk shouting encouragement and baring their breasts. Although the German and Scandinavian societies of that period have a masculine image, Tacitus claims that women enjoyed an exalted position. The Germani believed that women possessed an inherent holiness and a natural gift of prophecy. Therefore their advice was eagerly sought on matters of importance to the tribe.

On major matters an assembly of the chiefs of each clan was called to discuss the situation. These assemblies took place after the new or full moon. These dates were regarded as auspicious by the Germani who, says Tacitus, reckoned the passing of time by nights rather than days. This would seem to be a relic of the prehistoric matriarchal societies which flourished in ancient Europe. Each chief was allotted time at the assembly to state his views and if the people liked what they heard they clashed their swords. If they did not they shouted abuse. As well as self-governance, these assemblies meted out justice. Capital punishment was reserved for serious crimes such as murder or treason. Minor crimes were punished by fines of cattle or by confiscation of property. Part of the fines went to the High King and the rest was given to the victim of the crime or his or her relatives. Democratically, the assembly elected magistrates who administered justice on a local level in the villages. They were assisted by representatives elected from among the people. Although all the Germani had the right to bear arms, the assembly had to be satisfied that the bearer was competent enough to use them before such permission was granted.

The universal daily costume in Germany at the time of Tacitus' visit was a large cloak fastened with a brooch. In cold weather they also wore thick animal pelts. Women's dress consisted of the simple cloak and a sleeveless undertunic of linen or wool. Although Tacitus does not mention jewellery, we know from the archaeological evidence of the Saxon colonization of England that the Germani wore ornaments showing considerable craftmanship.

In contrast to the sexual licence prevalent in Rome, Tacitus regarded the Germans as a moral people. He states that the men were unique among non-Roman peoples in having only one official wife. There were a few exceptions, such as those of high political rank who for reasons of state had to take other wives in order to forge alliances. Marriage gifts were exchanged between the two families as a ritual act to court the favour of the gods ruling fertility. Tacitus obviously regarded the Germani as puritanical by Roman standards. However, there is evidence that the German and Scandinavian people regarded the sexual act as an act of worship of the life force. One of their most important seasonal festivals was in early spring when a man and woman representing the god and goddess of fertility ritually mated. Folk memories of this spring festival survived into the Christian period as May Day which, despite the protests of outraged clerics, often involved blatant sexual symbolism and erotic games.

The Germani apparently had a very healthy social life. Tacitus related that no other nation had such an appetite for feasting. It was regarded as a serious insult to turn a traveller away from the door. He or she would be invited in and given the finest food and drink available. No distinction was made between friends and strangers so far as hospitality was concerned. In contrast to the rich fare on Roman tables, the food at Germanic feasts was simple. It consisted largely of fresh meat, wild fruits, curdled milk and barley wine.

With the decline of Roman imperial power, the expansion of the Germanic tribal kingdoms began. We are taught at school that after the fall of the Roman Empire Europe descended into a barbaric Dark Age which was only enlightened by the teachings of medieval Christianity. As we have seen, the tribal people of Europe, both the Germani and the Celts, possessed a civilized form of society which was envied by some Romans. Although the domination of England by the Saxons is regarded as a warlike act, it did not begin that way. The sixth-century monk Gildas, who witnessed the end of the Pax Romana, observed that the Germani were admitted into Britain 'like so many wolves into a sheepfold'. Originally, Saxon mercenaries were invited to Britain by the Romano-Celts to defend the native population from raids by Norse pirates.

Another monk, Bede, writing in the eighth century CE stated that the earliest settlers invited to England were the Saxons, Angles and Jutes. Some Germani had been brought to Britain by the Romans as they had a policy of recruiting soldiers from the lands they had conquered. Even before the withdrawal of the Roman legions Saxon raiders had made sporadic attacks on the English coast. In 367 CE the Saxons, allied with the Picts and the Scoti, had invaded northern England. Several Saxon settlements are known to have been established in the south of Britain during the last days of the Roman occupation.

In 428 CE the Saxon warlords Hengist and Horsa, who seem to have also been priests of a sacred horse cult, were invited to Britain to help safeguard it against outside attack. The two Saxons arrived with several ships packed with armed troops. When eventually the British rulers asked the Saxons to leave the situation became open warfare. In

495 CE the Romano-Celtic leader Arthur won several victories against the Saxons but was eventually killed in battle. With him died the last organized resistance to the establishment of Saxon kingdoms in southern England.

Although there is evidence of Christian shrines in Roman Britain, the invading Saxons were still predominantly pagan. There is ample evidence that the use of the Runes was well established among the Saxon invaders. The seax or short sword was carried by most German warriors. Some of these weapons, especially those blessed in a sacred grove, were believed to possess magical powers. Such swords can be easily identified because they had an amber bead or piece of rock crystal inlaid in the hilt. Amber was regarded as a very sacred stone by the ancient pagans. Magical weapons of this type were given personal names such as Stormbringer or Enemyslayer by their owners. They were believed to have an independent existence, fed by the life force of the enemies they killed.

Some of these magical swords were engraved with Runes. One famous example is a sixth-century seax unearthed in Faversham in Kent. On it is the runic letter Tyr in the shape of an arrow pointing heavenwards. This Rune is specifically associated with the war god Tyr or Tiw. It is obvious that the sword had been dedicated by its owner to the god of war in a religious ceremony. Any warrior who carried Tiw's Rune on his sword was ensured of victory. According to an old Norse poem (see p. 45), anyone who wished to become skilled in the martial arts should become conversant with the Rune of war. The name of Tiw should be cut on the hilt of his sword, on the back of the blade and twice on the 'shining side'.

Two other examples of runic carved weapons are worth noting. One is an iron sword found on the Isle of Wight. Engraved on the silver scabbard is a runic inscription reading 'Woe to the weapons of the foe' and 'Increase to pain', which is a chilling description of the sword's potential. Another archaeological find has been described as the Rosetta Stone of Runelore. This was the broken blade of a seax dredged up from the River Thames in 1857. It has on it the complete runic alphabet together with a word in Runes believed to be the name of the owner. Experts believe the sword may have been made in Kent and date it from the ninth century CE.

Just as the Germani had begun their colonization of Britain by coastal raids, so, as the Saxon kingdoms were established, the first major attacks by the Norsemen or Vikings began. In order to understand the influence of the Vikings in early medieval Europe we must identify the distinct Viking Age. It lasted from 800 to 1000 CE. During this period the Vikings had regular trading links with the Middle East. They dealt in precious stones and furs, which they used to open trade routes to the Far East including India. Through these contacts Arabian silver and silk flowed back into Northern and Western Europe. When this international trading market collapsed because of wars in Russia and the Middle East, the isolated raids by Norse pirates were replaced by full-scale invasions of the European coastal areas by large numbers of heavily armed warriors.

The best known of these attacks in English history is the raid on the monastery at Lindisfarne in Northumberland in 793 CE. It is this raid which provides us with the popular image of the Viking as a long-haired rapist in a horned helmet. The raid had been preceded by omens of doom. According to *The Anglo-Saxon Chronicle*, there had been whirlwinds, thunderstorms and the sighting of dragons in the sky before the Viking attack. It was generally believed by the monks that the looting and destruction of Lindisfarne was a punishment by God for the sins of the people. The monks do not specify what sins these were, but they were either of a sexual nature or the survival of pagan practices.

From the ninth century the Viking raids intensified. In 839 a large group of Norwegian raiders invaded Ireland and attempted to replace the Christian religion with the worship of the thunder god Thor. However, in 844 the Viking leader was captured by the Irish and drowned. By the end of the ninth century large areas of northern England and southwest Scotland were under Viking rule. By the tenth century the Vikings had been granted land in northern France in exchange for a promise to stop their raids and had occupied Saxon strongholds in southern England.

The Norsemen achieved these successes because they had an organized society. In Scandinavia the Viking social structure was as sophisticated as any in contemporary Europe. Villages were built around greens, as in later medieval style, and there were large farms producing food for both their owners and the local community. In the period 950–1050, when the trading links across Europe had finally collapsed, the concept of the centralized state replaced that of the rural society. This involved the creation of a strong aristocracy, with tribal chiefs drawn from the warrior class and wealthy landowners. There were three main social classes in Viking society. The highest was the king but, as we have seen in Germanic society, he was not an absolute ruler and was answerable to the people. Next to the king were the earls, who were landowners and merchants. The eldest sons of this class inherited their estates and carried on the family line. In an old Icelandic poem it is said that the eldest son of such a family rode hunting with the hounds, was a skilled swordsman, was an expert with the Runes, which he uses to blunt the weapons of his enemies, calm the waves, put out flames and vanquish grief. The most important social group, however, was the working class, which comprised tenant farmers, blacksmiths, tool and weapon makers, artists and hunters.

It would be incorrect to regard either the Saxons or the Norsemen as 'uncivilized barbarians'. Certainly they had not attained the same level of technological expertise as found in European society in the later medieval period. However, they possessed a democratic social structure and had a highly developed moral awareness. While the raids on the British coastland by both the Saxons and the Vikings were bloody events, they pale into insignificance when compared with even the most minor wars or terrorist outrages experienced today.

As we have seen in this brief history, the people of Northern Europe who used the Runes were not mindless savages driven onward by blood lust. They were the product of a complex social organization which was committed to grassroots democracy and community politics. It is unfortunate that the present-day image of the Vikings popularized by inaccurate Hollywood movies has brainwashed the public into accepting a sensational picture of life during the period when the Runes were in general use.

2

In our first chapter we examined the known historical origin of the Runes and the lifestyles of the Northern European peoples who used them. We must now step into the realm of mythology, legend and magic to discover the spiritual roots of the runic system and how they relate to the ancient religious concepts of pagan Europe.

Although the Runes probably developed from prehistoric rock symbols, according to their mythical history they were a gift from the gods to Odin. The name Odin has a confusing etymology. It has been derived from the Old Norse root word *od*, meaning either 'wind' or 'spirit'. Another version from Old Norse is Voden which in Old High German translates as Woden or Wotan. This has been associated with the name of an Indo-European sky god known as Wodenaz. This word in turn has been compared with the Sanscrit *vata* and the Latin *ventus*, meaning 'wind'. Odin or Woden can therefore be identified as a wind or storm god who took on some of the attributes of the ancient Indo-European sky god.

He was a god associated by his worshippers with the elemental powers of nature, the eternal cycle of death and rebirth and arcane sources of magical wisdom. He possessed the power to raise the dead, divine the future, change his shape at will and fly through the sky. Odin is the archetypal shaman.

Physically we can visualize Odin as a tall, thin man wearing a long, dark cloak. His grey hair falls in tangled locks to his shoulders and he has only one eye which burns bright blue. The gaping socket from which his missing eye was torn is hidden by the wide brim of a soft hat pulled down over one side of his gaunt face. He leans on a blackthorn staff and is guarded by familiar spirits in the form of a raven and a wolf. As an accomplished shapeshifter, Odin can appear in many different guises but it is in human form that he is encountered by travellers on lonely tracks or at crossroads where gallows stand.

Unlike other gods, Odin frequently visits the world of humankind. It is reported that he materialized to the Danish king Harald Wartooth. Odin made a solemn promise to the king that he would grant him immunity from wounds if the ruler would dedicate to him all the souls of those he killed in battle. Naturally Harald was pleased to give such an oath, but Odin, displaying the fickle mood for which he is famous, broke his promise. The god created enmity between Harald and his close friend King Ring. Odin gave Ring the details of a special battle formation. When the Danish king rode into battle he found Odin beside him in the chariot. Harald begged one more favour from the one-eyed god, promising him the soul of every warrior killed in the battle. In reply Odin laughed and hurled the king from the vehicle so that he died.

The belief that Odin was not a god who could be trusted was widespread. He was regarded as a cunning adversary, a trickster and a god who often broke the promises he made to his mortal followers. In the old Norse sagas there are many references to Odin's oath breaking, his trickery and two-faced attitude. It is even possible that some of the later medieval stories about people being double-crossed by the Devil after exchanging their souls for riches were based on Odin's reputation as a trickster. When Christianity eliminated the old paganism the gods of the Ancient Faith became devils and demons. Many of the attributes of pagan gods like Odin were borrowed by medieval theologians to clothe their invented bogey Satan.

Odin was widely associated with death and especially with the warriors killed on the battlefield. One of Odin's many titles is the God of Battle, and as the Lord of Valhalla, the mythical Hall of the Slain, he welcomed the spirits of heroes killed in battle. His familiars, a wolf and a raven, are both creatures who feed on carrion. In the Norse poems Odin is depicted choosing dead warriors whom he will lead in the final battle of the gods at Ragnarok, the end of the world.

Many warriors invoked the help of Odin before battle. In the tenth century King Erik of Sweden successfully invoked Odin for a victory before a battle with his enemy Styrbion the Strong. Erik made a pact with the hooded god that he could possess his soul after ten years if he won the battle. Shortly after making this vow, the Swedish king met a tall, thin man with a hood pulled down to hide his face. This man, who was of course Odin in human form, gave Erik a thin stick. He told him to shoot this stick over the enemy army and cry out, 'Odin has you all.'

Erik obeyed these instructions and as soon as the magical stick left his hand it was transformed into a spear. As it sailed through the air above the enemy the whole army was struck blind. Unable to see, the frightened and confused men thrashed about wildly cutting each other with their swords. As the army fell in the blood of its self-inflicted

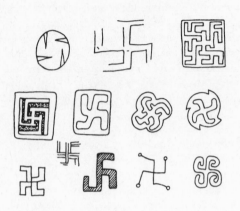

Saxon Burial Urns

St. Brigid's Fountain
Éire

Saxon brooch

Saxon; Sleaford, Lincs.

Isle of Man

Shutter slots.
Melbourn, Cambs.

British War
Savings Stamp.
circa 1916.

English heraldic

Medieval German.

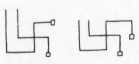

Jewish : Synagogue at Edd - Dikke

Mason's mark c.1450

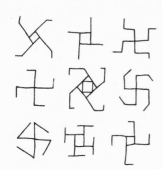

Celtic Interlace basic patterns

Vehmic Courts 'Thunderbroom'

Rosslau

English heraldic

Hungarian

From Bayley's 'Archaic England'.

Old German

Mark in Hereford Templar church.

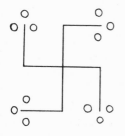

Smigorski

67th (Home Counties) Division emblem, British Army; Great War.

Finnish

wounds an avalanche began on the hillside above the troops. Unable to see the impending disaster, the enemy was crushed as the rocks tumbled down on them.

In his role as the God of Battle and guardian of the souls of the dead Odin was supported by the Valkyries. They were female spirits who appeared in the shape of Amazon-like warrior women: tall and strong with long, flowing hair and clad in battle armour. The Valkyries rode on horseback through the sky during a battle and carried the dead heroes across their saddles to Valhalla. The name Valkyrie is in fact a title and means 'Chooser of the Slain'. In Anglo-Saxon the word *valkyrie* is translated as *waelcyrge*, which has a similiar meaning. The *Waelcyrge* in Saxon folklore are represented as triple goddesses, akin to the Furies of Greek mythology.

As well as being conveyors of the souls of the dead to the Underworld, the Valkyries served at table in the Hall of the Slain. In one of the Norse sagas it is related that the Valkyries carry round the mead horns to make sure that the cups of the heroes are never empty. By the tenth century the Christian Church had succeeded in relegating them to the position of night hags or witches who rode at night causing evil.

In many ways the Valkyries had much in common with the Norns, the Scandinavian goddesses who weave the destiny of the human race. Visions of the Valkyries were often seen before battle. Before an eleventh-century battle in Ireland warriors reported seeing a group of dark-faced women in tattered grey cloaks weaving on a loom made from human entrails. A poem in one of the Norse sagas refers to this vision and quotes the words sung by the women, who are identified as Valkyries.

> We weave, we weave the web of the spear
> as on goes the standard of the brave,
> we shall not let him lose his life
> for the Valkyries have the power to choose the slain.
>
> All is sinister now to see,
> a cloud of blood moves over the sky
> the air is red with the blood of men
> as the battle women chant their song.

Other visions of the Valkyries are less detailed but no less relevant. One of the warriors of King Harold of Norway reported that just before he left to travel with the army to England in 1066 he had a prophetic dream. He saw a great witch wife [*sic*] standing on an island (England) with a fork in one hand and a trough in the other. He interpreted this as a sign that the army would be defeated. The witch wife would use the fork to rake up the corpses and fill the trough with their blood. Another warrior experienced a similiar dream which foretold doom for the Norwegian army. He saw a huge witch wife riding on a wolf in front of the English troops. The wolf carried in its jaws the body of a man from whom blood dripped. As the wolf consumed one body the old witch wife threw another for it to eat. The Norwegians, of course, met in battle with King Harold of England at Stamford Bridge in 1066 and were decimated. Harold marched south to meet his own destiny against the Normans, descendants of Norsemen, at the Battle of Hastings.

Led by Odin, the Valkyries riding across the night sky are the source of many of the European folktales concerning the Wild Hunt. Traditionally, this is a host of demonic figures on horseback led by a wild huntsman and accompanied by a howling pack of spectral hounds. The Wild Hunt rides across the countryside searching for lost souls and in the Christian period was said to be led by the Prince of Darkness. In pre-Christian times the Celts believed the Wild Hunt was led by Gwyn-ap-Nudd, the magician god of the Underworld, who rode out from Glastonbury Tor in Somerset. In Celtic mythology the tor was a hollow hill and one of the entrances to the Otherworld of spirits and faeries. In the early medieval period the Wild Hunt was believed to have been led by Odin and among his host he numbered Valkyries, woodland sprites, dead warriors from Valhalla and elves. As Christianity made its influence felt on folklore traditions, the wandering souls of the unbaptized and suicides were added to the ghostly company.

As leader of the Wild Hunt the hooded god Odin or Woden rode his mythical horse called Sleipnir. This magical beast was grey in colour and had eight legs. This fact prompted the Norse riddle: 'Who are the two that ride the Thing. Three eyes they have together, ten feet and one tail and thus they travel through the land.' In some parts of Germany the Wild Hunt was led by a mysterious female goddess figure known as Frau Wode. She seems to have been a feminine version of Woden and rode a white horse. Her appearance was said to be a sign of good fortune and prosperity, which is in direct contrast to the usual symbolism of the Wild Hunt as an omen of death. In northern France, settled by Norse pirates, the Wild Hunt was led by the goddess Hel and was known as Mesnée à Hellequin.

The Wild Hunt is often glimpsed in a winter storm by superstitious peasants. The howling of the wind or the cries of migrating geese have been interpreted as the howling of the demon hounds. One can imagine that such sounds would be regarded by simple country folk as harbingers of doom. It was widely believed that any late-night traveller unlucky enough to encounter the hunt would die in a short while. Frequently the Wild Hunt ran down travellers foolish enough to be out on the roads after sunset. If you saw the hunt approaching it was recommended that you hold on to a tree or large stone until it had passed. As the Wild Hunter and his host were visitors from the Other-world, presumably by holding on to a material object from this world you prevented them from harming you. In some cases Woden would show mercy to anyone standing in the middle of the road or at a crossroads. The cross is a significant symbol in Christian mythology, but crossroads were sacred to both Odin and the goddesses of death in paganism. This may offer some explanation for their role as safe refuges from the terror of the Wild Hunt. Crossroads were often associated with the Wild Huntress Holda. She would advise the hapless traveller that her horse had gone lame and reward those who assisted her with a trifling gift which the foolish might throw away. Those who kept her gift would find by the time they returned home that it had been transformed into solid gold.

Perhaps the most famous example of the Wild Hunter is Herne who haunts Windsor Park in Berkshire. This medieval English folk character has been identified with both Woden and the Celtic stag god Cernunnos. According to the legend, during the resign of Henry VIII a keeper named Richard Herne was accused of poaching deer from the royal herd. Rather than face the punishment meted out for such an offence Herne hanged himself from a blasted oak in Windsor Forest. Ever since then his ghost has haunted the vicinity of the oak and a small glade nearby, evocatively called the Faeries' Dell.

Herne the Hunter must have been a terrifying sight in the thick gloom of twilight, which was his favourite hunting time. He always wore a strange helmet made from a stag's skull and decorated with antlers. On his left wrist he had an iron bracelet which glowed with an eerie light. An owl flew above him as he led his pack of ghoulish hounds through the woods. Interestingly, in some of the German legends of the Wild Hunt an owl called Tutosel flies before the ghostly host warning travellers of its approach. It has been claimed that Tutosel is a corrupted form of 'Tut Ursel' or 'Tooting Ursela'. She was a nun who joined the Wild Hunt after her death.

In a recent edition of the occult magazine *Quest* Sid Birchby, who has made an extensive study of the Runes, suggested that Herne the

Hunter might be associated with the Rune Cen. The meaning of this Rune is 'torch' and specifically a pine torch. Birchby links this with Herne's obvious symbolism as a woodland god. He notes that both 'torch' and 'torque' derive from the same root word meaning 'something which is twisted'. Torques are gold neck collars and are found in the graves of both Saxon and Celtic warriors; they were a symbol of high rank. On the famous Gundestrup ritual cauldron unearthed in Sweden a horned stag god is depicted sitting crosslegged, surrounded by animals. In his hand he holds a torque over the animals as a symbol of his power. The stag god on the Gundestrup cauldron, says Birchby, is the Master of Animals and the Lord of Forests. He holds aloft the torque as a sign of his dominion over the forces of nature and is the Indo-European prototype of Herne/Woden/Cernunnos, who leads the Wild Hunt.

Odin's other major attribute, apart from rulership over the Otherworld and the powers of death, is wisdom. The Romans when they encountered the worship of Odin or Woden equated him with their deity Mercury. In classical Roman mythology the god Mercury, or Hermes, was the messenger of the gods of Olympus. He was also the god of commerce, trade, communication, travel and education. Mercury possessed special winged sandals and a winged helmet which granted him the magical ability to fly. He was also the guide of the souls of the dead to the Underworld. In ancient Egyptian myths Mercury was equated with both the ibis-headed god of wisdom Thoth (pronounced Tehuti) and the jackal-headed god of the dead Anubis.

Although the Romans, like all pagan people, tolerated the worship of the native gods of whatever country they conquered, they had the ethnocentric habit of equating foreign gods with their own pantheon. In some respects this practice has proved useful for it has helped to identify the individual characteristics of many Celtic and Germanic deities. However, it has also meant that we have lost many of the original names of the native gods and goddesses in the process. Their comparison of Odin/Woden and Mercury is understandable. Odin is regarded as either the inventor or discoverer of the Runes. This is a very Mercurian trait. The shaman god is also renowned for his habit of travelling the highways and byways of Europe, for his power to fly through the air and to change shape at will. He is often represented as a trickster or a cunning man and he can, as we have seen, be deceitful. Additionally, Odin is the guardian of the Underworld and a guide to the dead. All these attributes would have naturally suggested to the Romans that Odin was a North European version of Mercury.

An explicit link between Odin and Mercury is given in the following tenth-century poem. It is obviously Christian in outlook and reflects a cynical disbelief in the efficacy of the old pagan gods.

> Once there lived a man who was Mercury called,
> he was vastly deceitful and cunning in his deeds,
> he loved well to steal and all lying tricks,
> the heathens had made him the highest of the gods,
> and at crossroads they offered him booty,
> and to the high hills
> brought him victims to slay,
> this god was most honoured among all the heathens,
> his name when translated to Danish was Odin.

Another example of the correspondence between Odin and Mercury is revealed by an examination of the names for the days of the week, which, in English, are derived from the principal Nordic gods. Wednesday is in fact a corruption of Woden's Day. The Romans called that day after Mercury, and when the Saxons adopted the Roman calendar they translated Mercury's Day directly into Woden's Day, suggesting that so far as they were concerned the two gods were identical.

Odin is said to have lost an eye because he sacrificed it to the god Mimir, the giant guardian of the holy well of wisdom in the Otherworld. Only by sacrificing his eye could Odin drink from the well and gain wisdom. To gain the wisdom of the Runes Odin had to make the supreme sacrifice. He hung on a tree, allegedly the sacred World Tree, for nine days and nine nights impaled on his own spear. This extraordinary event is allegedly recounted in Odin's own words in one of the sagas.

> I trow that I hung on the windy tree
> swung there nights all nine
> gashed with a blade
> bloodied for Odin
> myself an offering to myself
> knotted to that Tree
> no man knows whither the roots of it run
>
> None gave me bread
> None gave me drink
> Down to the depths I peered
> to snatch up Runes
> with a raging scream
> and fell in a dizzied swoon

Wellbeing I won and wisdom too
I grew old and joyed in my growth
from a word to a word
I was led to a word
from a deed to another deed.

A shortened, Christianized version of this poem also survives in an old Anglo-Saxon charm which involves the gathering of nine herbs.

Thyme and fennel, a pair great in power
the wise Lord, holy in heaven,
wrought these herbs while hung on the cross,
he placed them and put them in the nine worlds,
to aid all, rich and poor.

At first glance you might be mistaken for thinking that the term 'wise Lord' and the phrase 'hung on the cross' are straightforward references to Jesus of Nazareth. In fact the reference to 'the nine worlds' gives the game away, for these are the nine heavens or planes of existence recognized by Norse cosmology. The 'wise Lord' is in fact Odin, who hung on the cosmic World Tree to gain the secret wisdom of the Runes. From contemporary accounts we know that the rites of the Odinist cult were often connected with the symbolism of hanging on a tree. There are grim travellers' tales of human sacrificial victims who were stabbed and then hanged from trees around the temples of Odin. Roman historians record that in parts of Scandinavia and Iceland (a Nordic province) the first prisoner captured in a war was sacrificed to Odin by this method. Although we rightly condemn this practice, it is not that many years ago that the public hanging of prisoners for minor offences was a feature of our own Christian society.

If the hanging of Odin on a tree and his subsequent torment seem a little strange for a god to endure, it is worth considering the theory that the original Odin/Woden was a mortal human being. It has been suggested that in the first century of the Christian period Sig, the chief of the Aesir, who were an Asiatic tribe, emigrated from the Caspian Sea in Northern Europe. Sig travelled northwest from the Black Sea to Russia, where he placed one of his sons as ruler. Two other sons were to become rulers of the Saxons and the Franks. He then advanced to Denmark, setting up yet another son as ruler, and then entered Sweden. In that country the king became a convert to the sacred mysteries taught by the stranger and eventually gave up his throne to him.

Sig changed his name to Odin and established a kingdom which included the whole of Scandinavia. He ruled this kingdom with the assistance of a priesthood of twelve elders, who represented the twelve Zodiac signs. After his death the historical Odin was deified, a common enough practice in pagan times. The mound where the historical Odin is said to be buried can still be seen near the site of the ancient Odinist temple at Uppsala in Sweden. It is possible that the original Odin was a Indo-European shaman who migrated from his Asian homeland to Northern Europe and founded a new religion based on the mystical symbols of the Runes. Certainly there is historical evidence that Odinism was not imported into Germany and Scandinavia until the late Iron Age. It replaced the aboriginal Bronze Age religion which worshipped a pantheon of gods and goddesses of fertility.

The American occultist Manley Palmer Hall has written extensively on the Odinist mysteries. He claims that these mysteries were enacted as ritual dramas in the style of the classical mystery cults of Greece and Rome but in nine underground caves. Nine was a sacred number in Norse and German mythology and represented the nine levels of existence in the universe. Palmer categorized these nine worlds or heavens as follows: *Asgard*, the heaven world of the elder gods; *Alfheim*, the world of light and the beautiful elves; *Niflheim*, the world of cold and darkness in the north; *Joltonheim*, the world of the giants situated in the east; *Midgard*, the world of the human race in the middle place or Middle Earth; *Vanaheim*, the world of the Vanes, which is located in the west; *Muspellsheim*, the world of fire, located in the south; *Svartalfaheim*, the world of the dark elves, which is under the earth; and *Helheim*, the world of the dead, which is at the lowest point of the universe. Helheim was a prototype of the Christian Hell although there is no evidence that the Odinists regarded it as a place of punishment.

It should be understood that under normal circumstances these nine worlds, with the exception of Middle Earth, were invisible to the five senses of human beings. During initiation the spirit of the candidate was liberated from its physical vehicle by the occult techniques of the priests of Odin and wandered freely through the nine worlds. According to Hall, the candidate seeking entry into the Odinist mysteries was given the task of raising Odin's son Baldur from the dead. In Norse myth the death of Baldur was caused by the god Loki. Hall claims that, although the initiate was not aware of the fact until the end of the ceremony, he or she was in fact playing the role of the dying god Baldur.

Each cave the initiate passed through represented not only one of the nine worlds or heavens but also one of the many spheres of nature.

Eventually the initiate emerged through a maze of passageways into the final cave. Facing him or her was a statue of the beautiful young god Baldur. In this inner sanctum the initiate recited an oath of secrecy to protect the teachings of the Odinist mysteries from outsiders, kissed the naked blade of a sword and drank a special draught of mead from a human skull. He or she was then given a silver ring engraved with runic characters and informed that as a result of travelling through the nine worlds he or she had been reborn as a perfected human being and a disciple of Odin.

If Manley Palmer Hall's version of the Odinist rites can be accepted, then we have in the Northern European religion practices which are comparable to the mysteries of classical Rome, Greece and Egypt. The initiate is revealed not only as the human representative of Baldur in his symbolic journey through the nine worlds of creation, but comes face to face with the young god at the climax of his sacred quest. This is a magico-spiritual practice common to many pagan initiatory rites in the classical and pre-classical world. In some of these ceremonies the candidate travelled through a ritual maze. At its centre he found himself facing a huge mirror reflecting back his own image. This was a simple yet very effective method of teaching the initiate the meaning of the immortal words carved above the gate of the Delphic oracle in ancient Greece: 'Man, Know Thyself'. It taught the important spiritual lesson that the real truth cannot be found outside in the material world but must be encountered within. The quest is the method used to send the seeker into the outer world that he or she may realize the truth within. Symbolically, the initiates into the Odinist mysteries were representing the god Baldur, but when they entered the last cave and came face to face with the god they were facing their own inner selves.

The sacred quest is an important aspect of initiation into any form of spiritual or mystical mystery. Odinism has its theological roots in the universal shamanistic religion which was prevalent in pre-Christian Europe. During the initiation ceremonies practised by shamans the neophyte travels in spirit form to the Underworld. In many cultures this Underworld is a mirror image of our material world. The trees grow downwards, the sun sets in the east and rises in the west, and rivers flow backwards. An important part of the pre-initiatory experience which grants the cloak of the shaman to the neophyte is a period of isolation. This period often involves spiritual experiences during which the neophyte may contact the spirits of his or her dead ancestors, nature spirits or the culture gods of his or her religion. Although Hall describes the mysteries of Odin taking place in subterranean cave temples, it seems probable that prior to this initiation the candidate may have undergone enforced isolation. During this period his or her spirit would have been liberated from the physical body, possibly by the use of hallucinogenic drugs such as the sacred mushroom fly agaric or by occult techniques known to the priests of Odin.

We have seen that the historical Odin, if he existed, was associated with an archetypal priesthood of twelve wise adepts. Manley Palmer Hall claims these adepts represented the twelve signs of the Zodiac. When Iceland was colonized by the Norwegians they established the Allthing or assembly where twelve magistrates or local rulers held court and administered justice. There was no king ruling Iceland at that period but his place was taken by the Lawspeaker. His role was to recite the codex of the law and pronounce final judgement at the end of each session which was governed by the twelve wise ones. At a paper read before the British Association in 1947 Mary Daielli suggested that the Allthing was a secular copy of the rulership of Valhalla by Odin and his twelve gods.

In her paper Daielli refers to the fact that in Scandinavian and Teutonic mythology Odin is often featured with two other gods, forming a divine triad. This triple aspect is linked with the Norse mythic concept of the universe in its pre-creation state being divided into zones of fire and ice. In between these two extremes is a meeting point where the cosmic fire and ice are in balance. This is Midgard or Middle Earth, the home of humanity. This divine triad, Daielli suggests, was transposed to the administration of the Allthing. In the local Icelandic courts it was customary for each magistrate to be assisted by two others. Any verdict they reached would be as a result of tripartite discussion.

Odin was also associated with the religious idea of sacred or divine kingship. In his book *The Cult of Kingship in Anglo-Saxon England* William A. Chaney claims that the German and Anglo-Saxon (English) royal houses believed they were directly descended from Woden. According to Tacitus, often the kings of the Germani were also priests who practised the state rites of the pagan Old Religion. The king was the high priest of the tribe or, to use his official title, the Warden of the Holy Temple. He performed the sacrifices for good crops and victory in battle. He divined the portents for the future by casting the Runes. But if the king failed to deliver what he had promised the people might decide that the gods had forsaken him. In such circumstances they were within their rights to replace the loser with another, stronger, candidate. It is recorded that when King Olaf of Sweden failed to perform the proper sacrifices and fertility rites to ensure a good harvest his loyal subjects burned him alive in his own house as an offering to Odin.

According to Chaney, the king and the royal family were possessed of a special magical power in the eyes of their people. This power was granted to the German and Anglo-Saxon royal houses because of their unique position as tribal high priests and their hereditary lineage reaching back to Woden. Chaney points out that the prefix *os* occurs in the names of twelve Northumbrian kings. This is significant because *os* means 'god' or 'divine' in Old Icelandic/Norse. It is also the name of one of the Runes which is dedicated to Odin. Chaney refers to the tradition in Sweden that queens not kings were originally accepted as representatives of the deities of the Norse pantheon. The queens represented the goddess of fertility Freya. The kings represented her consort Frey, the god of fertility. Although Nordic religion in general has always been regarded as male-orientated, it is a fact that the original objects of worship by the Scandinavian peoples were a pantheon of fertility gods led by the Great Mother Goddess. It was only in late historical periods that the male sky gods grew in influence and challenged the worship of the Great Goddess.

In pagan times the coronation of the monarch was a sacred religious rite for it conferred on him or her divinity. In modern times vestiges of this survive in the coronation service used to crown the British monarch. This ceremony is performed in Westminster Abbey with all the bishops of the Church of England and representatives of the state political parties present. The coronation rite is presided over by the Archbishop of Canterbury who is the state high priest. In a ritual with heavy pagan overtones the king or queen is anointed with sacred oil, presented with 'magical' symbols (i.e. the sceptre, orb and crown) and blessed by the high priest of the nationally recognized religious faith.

Traditionally, then, Woden or Odin is a god of warriors and kings. He is the god who leads his warriors into battle and carries their souls off to heaven when they die. Woden was also regarded by some of the German tribes as the god of the harvest. This may be a confusion with the phallic god Frey whose major festival was celebrated at the time of the harvest. The association of Woden with the harvest has survived into relatively modern times in the belief that Wednesday or Woden's Day is lucky for sowing or growing crops.

Although it was widely believed by the common people that the rulers of the Saxon royal house were descended from Woden/Odin, in the medieval historical chronicles compiled by monks it is stated that the kings were related to biblical characters such as Noah and even Jesus. This was a blatant attempt by the Church to suppress the origins of the Saxon royal family as divine priest kings descended from the hooded god of the Runes.

3

Although the Runes were mostly linked with magic and ancient knowledge, in practice they had many uses both sacred and secular. Each Rune had a special meaning and symbolism and either singly or in groups could be used in magical charms. Originally their purpose was as a key to the pagan religious system of the North European people and as a method of divination. However, their use in magical workings meant that you had birth Runes, health Runes, death Runes, fertility Runes, weather Runes, love Runes and cursing Runes. Some of these uses will become apparent as we study the runic alphabet in more detail, but some indication of their magical uses can be given now.

Runes were often used to protect burial mounds from looters. They were carved on special standing stones which were either placed inside the tomb or at its entrance. Such Runes had to be carved at night and without the use of iron tools. This seems to be a product of superstition, but these special instructions are in accordance with ancient magical tradition. It is obvious that any ritual of a necromantic nature, even one protecting the dead from harm, should be performed during the hours of darkness. It is during these hours that the divine forces which have rulership over death and the Underworld are at their strongest. According to popular folk belief, iron was the only metal with the power to fend off the spirits of the departed (not all of whom were friendly towards humans) and the elven folk. The use of iron was expressly forbidden in the sacred groves used for pagan worship or near burial mounds where the bodies of the tribe's ancestral dead had been laid to rest.

The widespread ancient belief in the magical power of iron to have a negative influence on spiritual forces and the taboo of its contact with religious sites may date back to the Bronze Age. Then the Aryan people who used iron weapons conquered the aboriginal tribes who still used bronze for crafting their weapons and tools. The small, dark-skinned Bronze Age folk were regarded by the tall, fair invaders as faeries or magicians with supernatural powers. The superstitious belief soon arose that the Bronze Age people were scared of iron. There would have been an element of truth in this, for an iron sword could slice through the relatively soft bronze blades of the conquered tribes. The confusion between the Bronze Age people and the elven folk gave rise to the idea that elemental spirits could be controlled by iron. Such an idea offers one explanation for the use of magical swords by medieval sorcerers to summon and subdue demons.

Another little-known attribute of the Runes was their power to allow prisoners to escape their chains. Writing in the late seventh century CE, Bede relates the story of a Northumbrian prisoner who managed to undo his chains and escape captivity. When he was eventually recaptured his captors asked him how he had achieved escape and posed the question: 'Do you know of the loosening Runes and do you have the [magical] letters written about you?' This power of the Runes is referred to in a poem about Odin and his use of the runic characters. He allegedly says:

> This fourth runic skill I know,
> if men put fetters on my limbs
> I chant such a charm that will
> let me escape from them.

The Havamal

We have already described how warriors engraved the Runes on their sword blades and hilts. They also painted the Rune of the war god Tiw or Tyr on their shields. Such warriors often belonged to the special cult of Odin's followers known as the Berserkers. This word is derived from Old Norse and means 'bear shirt' or 'wolf skin'. It refers to the shaggy animal pelts worn in battle by these fearless stormtroopers of Odin. Apart from these animal skins, the Berserkers were naked and ran into battle screaming and howling like wild beasts. This bizarre behaviour led many people to believe that the Berserkers had the ability, shared with Odin, of being able to change their human form into the shape of animals.

Runes were also used for more mundane purposes by the warrior class to record the heroic deeds of those who went on overseas expeditions. Memorial stones were erected to commemorate Viking warriors who died fighting in raids overseas. In the later Viking Age these stones can be found engraved with both Runes and the Christian cross, testifying to the way the new religion took over the old paganism.

The varied use of the Runes by the Northern Europeans is illustrated by the following list taken from a Norse saga:

Runes of war know thee
if great thou wilt be
cut them on hilt of hardened sword
some on the brand's back
some on its shining side
twice the name of Tiw therein

Sea Runes good at need
learned for ship's saving
for the good health of
the swimming horse,
on the stern cut them
cut them on the rudder blade
and set flame the shaven oar,
how so big the sea hills
how so big the blue beneath
hail from the main and then
comest thou home.

Word Runes learn ye will
if thou wilt no man pay back
grief for the grief gavest,
wind thou these, cast thou these
all about ye,
at the Thing where folk throng
until the doom faring.

Of ale Runes know the wisdom
if thou wilt another man's wife
should not betray thine heart
that trusteth,
cut them on mead horn
on the back of each hand
and nicked upon the nail.

Help Runes shalt thou gather,
if skill thou would gain
to loosen mother from low lain child,
cut they be in hand's hollow
wrapped the joints round about
call for the Good Folk's gainsome help.

Learn the bough's Rune wisdom
if leechlore thou lovest
and wilt wot about wounds searching,
on the bark they be scored,
on the buds of trees
whose boughs look eastward ever.

Thought Runes shalt thou deal with
if thou wilt be of all men fairest
souled right and wise,
those creded, those first cut
those took first to heart.

On the shield they were scored that
stands before the Shining God,
on Early Waking's oar,
on All Knowing's hoof,
on the wheel which runneth,
on Sleipnir's jaw teeth,
on the sleigh's traces,
on the rough bear's paw,
on Bragi's tongue,
on the wolf's claw,
on the eagle's bill,
on bloody wings and badger's end,
on loosing palms and pity's path,
on glass and gold and goodly silver,
in wine and wort,
and the seat of the witch wife,
on Gungir's point,
and Grani's bosom,
and the Norn's snail,
and the neb of the night owl

All these so cut were shaven and
sheared and mingled with hold mead
and sent upon wide ways,
some abide with the elves,
some abide with the Aesir
or with the wise Vanir or
some still hold the sons of mankind.

These be the book Runes and
the Runes of good help
and all the ale Runes
and the Runes of much might
to whom so they may avail,
unbewildered, unspoilt,
they are whosesome to hear
thine thou with these then
when thou hast heard their lore
till the gods end their life days.

Various references in this poem from the Volsunga Saga can be allocated to specific Runes. For instance, in the first verse the poet is obviously taking the Tyr Rune sacred to the war god as his model. It was this Rune in the shape of an arrow which was engraved on the hilts and blades of swords belonging to Viking warriors. The sea Rune is Sigil and the word Rune is Os.

In verse nine we see that certain Runes are associated with the elves or the elemental realm of goblins, faeries and nature spirits, while others are linked with the Aesir and the Vanir. In Norse mythology the Aesir were the gods descended from Odin the Allfather. They were the Indo-European gods of destruction, storm and heaven. In the Nordic myths they seem to have been in conflict with the bright gods of fertility and the earth known as the Vanir, who were the deities of the Bronze Age Scandinavians.

The poem describes the different magical and secular uses of the Runes. They can be carved on the hulls of ships to protect them from being lost at sea, used to cure marital problems, ease childbirth, and they were even credited with the power to raise the dead. In one of the Norse sagas this ability is described as follows.

A twelfth spell I know
when I see aloft upon a tree
a corpse swinging from a rope
then I cut and paint Runes
so that the man walks
and speaks with me.

The Havamal

It is possible that the power of the Runes to raise the dead originated in the story of the shaman god Odin discovering their secret by hanging for nine days and nights on a tree. This is indicated in the above verse by the description of a corpse hanging on a tree which is an allusion to the ritual of self-sacrifice perpetuated by Odin in order to receive the wisdom of the Runes.

In addition to the use of Runes as magical charms, the primary usage of the magical alphabet was as a very effective method of divination. The practice of divining by the Runes was widespread among the ancient tribes of northern Italy and Germany. There are references to the runic oracle in the writings of both Plutarch and Julius Caesar. However, it is in the *Germania* of Tacitus that the most graphic account of the practice can be found.

Tacitus had a colourful career. He was a soldier, Roman senator, a

Odin by Ólafur Brynjúlfssons, from *Edda*, 1760. (Reproduced by permission of University College Library, London.)

historian and a colonial administrator of the Roman Empire. In the *Germania* he recounts the customs, geography and character of the German tribes who inhabited the country during the period when Rome was expanding its empire in the first century CE. He describes the use of Runes for divination in great detail. According to Tacitus, the Germans had a high regard for casting lots for divination. First, they cut a branch from a nut-bearing tree. This was carefully sliced into strips of equal size and length. These were then marked with the signs of the runic alphabet. Thus prepared, the Runes were cast at random on a white cloth. If the divination was of a public nature, then the rite was carried out by a state priest. If the consultation was private, then the head of the family read the Runes. Either way, the procedure was the same. After offering up a prayer to Odin the Runecaster looked up at the sky and selected at random three strips of wood carved with Runes. He or she then read the meanings of the Runes and offered guidance in accordance to what they foretold and the question asked.

Although all ancient peoples had their systems of divination, the Germans seem to have been obsessed with the subject. Tacitus relates how the priests kept special sacred white horses and divined the future by the noises they made. Their belief in omens is illustrated by the story about King Herod the Great's grandson, Herod Agrippa. He was thrown into prison for treason a few years after the execution of Jesus. On the first day he spent in prison an owl was seen to alight on a branch near his head. An old German prisoner saw this happen and told Herod Agrippa it was a lucky omen. He would soon be released and regain his previous high office. The German, however, also warned that when he saw the owl again he would die within five days. In due course the old man's prophecy came to pass and Herod was released from prison to become the Romans' puppet king in Judea. At the height of his power he went to the games in Rome. There, he was recognized as a god by his supporters. Suddenly Agrippa looked up and saw an owl flying across the ampitheatre towards him. He died in agony five days later from an unspecified stomach complaint.

As well as Tacitus', there are several other written accounts of divination which seem to relate to the casting of the Runes. In the epic story of *Beowulf* it is said that before the hero sailed for Denmark he 'observed the omens'. An Anglo-Saxon poet writing from a Christian viewpoint also refers to what is probably runic divination in the following poem concerning alleged cannabilistic tendencies among the unconverted pagans of his time.

Casting lots they let them decree
which should die first as food for the others
with hellish acts and heathen rites
They cast the lots and counted them out.

As we have seen from the account rendered by Tacitus, the casting of the Runes as a divinatory oracle was the task of the state priest; if he was not available or if the consultation was of a private nature, his place was taken by the tribal chief or the head of the family. The casting of the Runes was the special province of a priesthood who regarded themselves as blood kin to the hooded god Odin himself. Like the ancient priests of many of the old pagan cults, the Rune Masters or Mistresses, for there were priestesses as well as priests in paganism, were the spiritual descendants of the prehistoric shamans.

Shamanism is the oldest form of religious expression known to humanity. Before the emergence of the homocentric religions such as Buddhism, Islam and Christianity, which are centred on human prophets who preached a divine message, all forms of spirituality can be traced back to the shamanistic tradition. Shamanism originated in prehistoric times when the magician priests of the tribes performed magical rites to ensure that the hunters returned to the settlement with sufficient game to provide for the needs of the people or that the crops flourished so there was a good harvest. Gradually the shaman became the human mediator between the tribe and the gods, passing messages backwards and forwards. He or she was an inspired person or natural medium who could communicate with the Otherworld, acting as a two-way transmitter and receiver of divine intelligence.

In order to achieve this spirit communication with the realm of the gods the shaman had to be a person of extraordinary abilities. He or she had to be psychic or possess unusual physical attributes. Often the shaman would be a social outcast, possibly because of some physical disability. However, once the shaman's unique gifts had been recognized, he or she became an honoured member of the tribal unit even if he or she remained socially separated.

The shaman gained his or her magical powers and the ability to communicate with spirits through a self-initiation process. This involved an imaginative journey to the Otherworld where the shaman talked with the spirits of the dead and with the gods. Whether this event occurred as an actuality or was a psychological experience depends on your cultural viewpoint. The shaman achieved contact with the spirit world by using certain ancient occult techniques. These included ritual dancing, chanting and drum playing. Two of these techniques have a relationship to the Rune system. It has been pointed out that the ritual drums of the Finnish shamans had mystical symbols painted on them which resembled both the Runes and the prehistoric Hallristinger script. The chants used by the shamans were based on the magical language of animals which was a closely guarded shamanistic secret. It is known that this language was based on the cries of birds. In the German forms of runic magic the term used to describe an incantation is *galdr*, which is linked with bird song. In some prehistoric carvings and cave paintings shamans are shown wearing ritual bird masks.

As well as the occult techniques described above, the shaman achieved the liberation of the soul from the body, so that it could travel to the Underworld, by trance, prolonged periods of fast and sleeplessness, and sometimes by the use of natural drugs derived from hallucinogenic fungi which were prolific in the birch forests of Northern Europe. For the isolation period the shaman would withdraw to a remote place, such as the depths of a forest or a cave, and refrained from food for several days. During this self-initiation the would-be shaman received his or her mediumistic powers through the supernatural action of some natural object. This object might be a stone, a tree or an animal. This then became a ritual totem or power symbol for the shaman once he or she had completed the initiation and returned to the tribe.

An important aspect of the initiatory process which created a new shaman was the ritualistic ascent of a tree which represented the *axis mundi* or centre of the universe. A birch pole was set up in the middle of a woodland clearing and a small animal was sacrificed. Its blood was smeared on the base of the birch pole as an offering to the gods. Some of the blood was also smeared on the nine openings of the shaman's naked body, sealing it from possession by negative influences. Properly prepared, the shaman climbed the pole slowly, cutting nine notches in it with a ritual knife as he ascended. This symbolic journey represented in Norse and Germanic mythology the ascent of the soul through the nine worlds or heavens on the sacred World Tree known as Yggdrasil. The birch pole symbolized the pillar or World Tree, which was positioned at the mythological centre of the world and pointed up towards the North Star which was the stellar realm of the oldest gods known to humanity.

The Maypole, which was such a prominent feature of the medieval May Day festivities in both England and many European countries, may have had its origins in the pagan symbol of the World Tree. Huge wooden pillars known as Irminsuls were worshipped by Germanic tribes in pagan times. The ancient Slavs who occupied most of Russia and Eastern Europe in pre-Christian times worshipped huge wooden pillars carved at the top with the faces of their many gods. One of these Irminsuls was cut down by soldiers belonging to the army of Emperor Charlemagne in the eighth century CE. It is recorded that the destruction of the extensive pagan sanctuary surrounding the sacred pillar took at least three days to accomplish.

According to other contemporary accounts, a huge sacred tree was growing close to the temple dedicated to Odin at Uppsala in Sweden. This tree had gigantic branches hanging down to the ground and vast roots which spread out around it. According to the Christian writers of the pagan period, beside the sacred tree at Uppsala was a holy well in which human sacrifices were drowned to appease the gods.

The secret symbolism of the Maypole is said to be of a phallic nature. In folk belief the Maypole symbolizes the creative masculine force of the cosmos represented by the erect penis. The term 'Irminsul', used by the Saxons to describe the wooden pillar they revered, means 'a universal column which sustains everything'. If the Maypole is derived from the Irminsul, then its traditional phallic meaning is justified.

Odin/Woden was the archetypal shaman with the power to fly through the sky, raise the dead, divine the future and change shape into animal form. His many followers believed that these shamanistic abilities were a direct consequence of Odin's mystical experience on the World Tree which resulted in his gaining the secret knowledge of the Runes. Many Odinists believed they could obtain the same powers as Odin through the arcane study of the runic characters. In fact, Odin advised his worshippers exactly what they could expect to learn if they followed him on the shamanistic path.

> Ye shall find Runes and signs to read
> signs most mighty, signs so strong
> which the soothsayer coloured,
> the High Gods made
> and the Old Ones carved

He then posed four questions for the apprentice Rune Masters to answer.

> Do you know how they [the Runes] shall be carved?
> Do you know how they should be read?
> Do you know how they should be coloured?
> Do you know how they should be tried?

This type of ritual question and answer would have featured in the secret rites used to initiate a priest or priestess of Odin. The candidate would have been expected to give the correct responses and prove to the initiator that he or she could provide a practical demonstration of Runecraft.

In general the Rune Master were selected from the ranks of the state priesthood who administered the national and local shrines dedicated to the pagan gods. In Sweden the priests were called the Atibba. An overseas visitor from Arabia, obviously on a trade mission, described these priests as having the authority of masters over the common people. The priests ordered the people to make sacrificial offerings of human beings, cattle and grain at the pagan temples. In Denmark the priests were called Thuls, meaning 'the reciters of incantations'. This was a reference to the priesthood's skill at Runecraft. As well as the state priests, there were also lay Rune magicians. In Scandinavia they were often described as Finns, which was a generalized term for the Lapplanders who settled in the region during the prehistoric period. The Finns were held in awe by the Norse people as accomplished shamans skilled in the magical uses of the Runes.

As we have noted earlier, these shamans were the spiritual descendants of the ancient priest magicians of the Stone Age and Bronze Age. Remains of these early shamans have been unearthed from Scandinavian burial mounds. A typical example is the burial uncovered at Lynberg near Copenhagen in the last century. Inside a roughly hewn oak coffin was found the skeleton of a magician together with his magical bag of tricks. This leather bag contained the stock-in-trade of a Bronze Age wizard (from Old English, meaning 'wise man') and included a number of amber beads; a conch shell, representing the female sexual organ; a falcon's claw, which would have granted him the power to fly; the bones of a snake, which is associated in pagan lore with the ability to heal the sick; a squirrel's tail; and the dried entrails of a rodent. That this was the burial place of a shamanistic magician was confirmed by the discovery of a forked hazel wand lying next to the body; such wands remain the primary magical tool of the shamanistic magician in the Western neo-pagan tradition.

Although most Rune Masters carried various magical charms and runic sigils, they could also be recognized quite easily because they adopted ritual costumes. Some wore headdresses made from the pelts of woodland animals such as foxes and badgers or deer complete with antlers. Others wore blue-dyed cloaks in honour of the colour traditionally sacred to Odin. As a staff of office the Rune Masters carried batons of ash, hazel, yew or oak carved with magical and runic signs. This type of ritual costume worn by folk magicians was widespread in ancient times. It is found in the annals of medieval witchcraft, which was a surviving remnant of the pagan Old Religion although heavily influenced by Middle Eastern beliefs imported into Western Europe during the Crusades.

In an article written for the journal of the Folklore Society the famous anthropologist Dr Margaret Murray describes the portrait of a male witch which was on display in the Sheffield Art Gallery. This painting dates from the seventeenth century and depicts a smiling, moon-faced man wearing a green hood with bells resembling the cap worn by court jesters. He is holding in his arms a brindle cat which is obviously supposed to be his familiar. Murray cites this painting as evidence of the high social position of wizards in England at the time when the portrait was completed.

Reginald Scot, writing in 1584, stated in his book *The Discoverie of Witches* that he knew of well-known witches who moved in upper-class circles and wore a special uniform so they could be recognized by potential clients. This was at a time when the persecution of witches was at its height. As late as the end of the last war it was recorded in East Anglia that local witches wore a ritual costume passed down through the generations. It consisted of three pieces of fur from weasels or polecats worn around the neck like a collar.

According to *The Saga of Erik the Red*, written in the thirteenth century CE, a person who divined the Runes in a professional capacity was recognizable by her distinctive costume. She wore a cloak set with stones around the hem. Around her neck and covering her head was a hood lined with white catskin. In one hand the Rune Mistress carried a staff with a knob on the end, and at her belt was a charm pouch. To complete the costume she wore catskin shoes and mittens.

Another of these Rune Mistresses is referred to in an Icelandic song composed by a seer who possessed the gift of prophecy.

Hedi men call me when their homes I visit
a far-seeing witch, wise in talismans
caster of spells, cunning in magic
to wicked women welcome always

Arm rings and necklaces Odin ye gave me
to learn my lore, to learn all magics
wider and wider through all worlds I see

Outside I sat myself when ye came
terror of Gods and gazed into my eyes

What do ye ask of me?
Why tempt me?

Odin I know where thy lost eye has gone
hidden away in Mimir's well
Mimir each morning his mead he drinks
Well, would ye know more?

There are coded references in the above song to various aspects of the training of the Rune Masters. From the first verse we can discern that Hedi is not a trained priestess of the state religion. She calls herself a witch, a caster of spells, a maker of talismans and a cunning woman who practises magic. It is evident that Hedi is a female shaman. In the second verse there are references to ritual jewellery – arm rings and necklaces – given to the witch by the hooded god himself. These sacred objects seem to possess magical powers and enable the witch clairvoyantly to visit the niṇe worlds or heavens of Nordic mythology. In the ancient Celtic, Nordic and Teutonic pagan religions the necklace or torque was a very important ritual object. Worn by the gods, it signified their divine status and was a symbol of spiritual and temporal power among their human worshippers. During the early 1950s archaeologists discovered the mummified bodies of several Iron Age human sacrifices which had been preserved in a Danish peat bog. Many of the victims were naked except for torques or leather nooses tied around their throats. This fact has led experts to suggest that the bodies were of sacrificial victims who were killed to honour the Great Mother Goddess. The wearing of neck rings or collars was a symbol that the wearer was subservient to the goddess of fertility.

At the beginning of the third verse of the song is a reference to the occult technique of projecting the astral body or spirit. Occultists believe we each have an astral double composed of spiritual material which is finer and less dense than the physical body. At times of sickness and stress or under special controlled conditions the astral double can be liberated from the physical body and can wander free. This technique would have been known to the priests and shamans who practised Runecraft.

The training to become a Rune Master or Mistress was both lengthy and strict. It had to be, for there were many dangers inherent in the Rune system for those who dabbled in its mysteries. Those who studied the ancient wisdom of the Runes seriously believed that each Runic letter was associated with an elemental spirit which, once evoked by the use of that Rune, had to be treated with respect. If one of these entities went out of control it could harm any human who came into contact with it. The Rune Masters believed, rightly or wrongly, that some of the elemental spirits evoked by the Runes were of the nature of incubi and succubi. These were medieval terms for spirit entities capable of having sexual intercourse with humans. Anyone who was possessed by one of these spirits became inflamed with an insatiable sexual desire which they were unable to control.

The training of Rune Masters was also strict because of the need for the Runecaster to know exactly what powers the Runes possessed. It is recorded that a well-known Rune Master named Egill was consulted by the relatives of a woman dying from a fever. Another magician skilled in Runecraft had already been consulted by the family. Despite his efforts on her behalf, the sick woman was no better. Because of his considerable knowledge of the Runes Egill discovered that the other magician had carved incorrect Runic letters on the whalebone he had hung over the dying woman's bed. In anger Egill condemned the uneducated Rune Masters who dabble with forces they cannot control and do not really understand.

> Runes shall not a man score
> save he can read them well
> that many a man betideth
> on a mirk stave to stumble
> saw I on a scraped whale bone
> ten dark staves scored
> thou hath to the leek widen
> over long sickness broughteth.

Egill scored out the incorrect Runes and engraved the proper ones on the bone. He then placed the healing charm under the sick woman's pillow and within a short time she awoke from her fevered sleep and eventually recovered her good health.

In another incident Egill used his runic knowledge to divine that his drink had been poisoned by an assassin hired by a rival magician. Egill carved a set of Runes around the rim of the cup which he suspected had been laced with a deadly poison. These Runes he reddened with his own blood from a cut in his arm. The cup immediately broke into pieces and the contents spilled all over the floor. According to Egill, if the drink had not been poisoned the Runes would not have had any effect.

When the Vikings ventured forth on their overseas expeditions they numbered among their ranks persons skilled in Runecraft. Possibly these were pagan priests or warriors who had studied the Runes before they took up arms. Evidence of the use of the Runes by Scandinavian seafarers can be found in the runic graffiti carved inside the megalithic burial chamber of Maes Howe in Orkney. In the winter of 1151 CE Viking pirates looted the site and left a runic inscription carved on the stones relating that they had carried off a great treasure. It is recorded in the runic graffiti that the Vikings returned in 1153 and they sheltered in the burial mound during a blizzard. During this storm two of the company apparently went insane but no reason is given for this odd event. One of the runic inscriptions boasts that 'the man most skilled in Runecraft west over the sea made these'. This person may not have been an accomplished Rune Master or priest of the cult of Odin but he obviously had a considerable knowledge of the runic alphabet.

The social position of the Rune Master in pagan Scandinavia and Germany was very important. Whether as an initiated member of the priesthood of Odin/Woden or as a self-initiated witch or shaman, the person skilled in Runecraft was widely respected and consulted, from the highest in the land to the humblest peasant. It was not until the coming of the new Middle Eastern religion of Christianity that the Runecaster's power and influence in the community was diminished. When the Church gained political power in the Middle Ages it soon exercised its newfound strength by eliminating the surviving vestiges of the pagan Old Religion. This suppression included the art of Runecraft. The Saxon abbot Aelric equated magic and the Runes in his sermon preached against what he called 'superstitions and popular customs' and during the medieval period the use or even the ownership of the runic alphabet was a serious criminal offence. In seventeenth century Iceland people who used the Runes for magic and divination were burned at the stake.

Despite this campaign of terror by the Christian Church to destroy the ancient wisdom of the Runes, considerable information survived the dark days of persecution. In the next section of this book we will be examining the practical aspects of rune lore, including making and casting Runes and their spiritual and divinatory meanings.

Part Two

THE RUNIC ORACLE

THE RUNIC ALPHABET

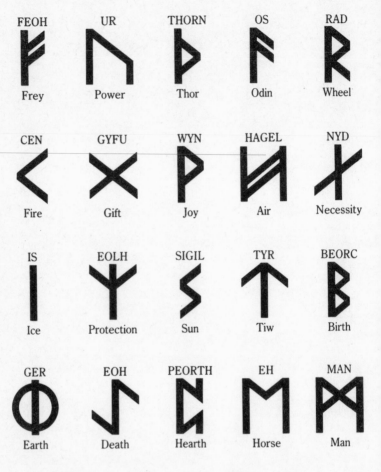

FEOH	UR	THORN	OS	RAD
Frey	Power	Thor	Odin	Wheel

CEN	GYFU	WYN	HAGEL	NYD
Fire	Gift	Joy	Air	Necessity

IS	EOLH	SIGIL	TYR	BEORC
Ice	Protection	Sun	Tiw	Birth

GER	EOH	PEORTH	EH	MAN
Earth	Death	Hearth	Horse	Man

LAGU	ING	DAEG	ODAL
Water	Fertility	Dawn	Ancestral

4

The ancient Rune Masters and Mistresses were trained for many years in the knowledge, wisdom and practice of the runic system. Their training was within the context of a spiritual framework embracing the highest philosophical ideals. It may seem strange to some readers that we use such terms to describe pre-Christian pagan beliefs. It may seem unacceptable to some modern religionists that the pagan Old Religion with its cosmic world view was more sophisticated in its reflection of spirituality than the extreme homocentric religious systems that dominated Europe in the Middle Ages. It had at least one main advantage over Christianity, for it was deeply rooted in the natural world and humanity's relationship with the universe. During the medieval period the Christian Church, in both its established and heretical forms, rejected nature and the material world as evil temptations which seduced the true believer from the spiritual path. The pagans recognized the dangers in ultra-materialism, but they had a more realistic view of nature, recognizing the role that humankind played in the cosmic wheel of life.

We explore the pagan philosophy of the Runes in relation to Norse and Teutonic religious beliefs in Part Three of this book. The purpose of this section is to examine the symbolism of the Runes and their practical use both as a method of divination and as a groundplan for spiritual progress. It is impossible for us to offer the reader the practical skills which would enable them to become a fully fledged Rune Master or Mistress. As we have seen, the training in Runecraft took many years of hard work. However, we are able to offer the interested seeker sufficient information to enable anyone to cast the Runes with enough expertise to provide answers to the problems of daily life for both themselves and others.

It must be stressed before we begin our study of the practical application of the runic alphabet that merely knowing the meaning of the Runes or possessing a set of Runes will not guarantee instant results. The Runes possess no inherent magical powers without some form of reaction from the user. Modern scientists have discovered that the secret of the universe which wise men and women have been seeking for thousands of years is *participation*. They now realize that it is the reaction of the observer who experiences the cosmos that creates reality. This self-created reality is sustained by an archetypal cosmos which exists beyond our space–time continuum. This is the realm of the gods spoken of in ancient mythology and legend. As a participant in the cosmic dance of life, it is the Runecaster's reaction to and with the Runes that provides the mechanism by which they work or do not work, as the case may be. The Runecaster and the Runes therefore become one synchronized unit which produces a flow of magico-spiritual energy leading to the desired result, i.e. a successful divinatory experience.

To a certain extent this is true of any form of divination. Today nearly every toyshop and stationer's sells Tarot cards and the advertising pages of magazines dealing with the occult and astrology are full of advertisements offering Tarot readings. This easy access has convinced many people that Tarot readings are a simple way to foretell the future. You need only to purchase a pack of Tarot cards, learn their meanings parrot fashion from one of the many instruction books on the market, and you are now equipped to do readings professionally. What the would-be Tarot readers do not realize is that, like the Runes, the Tarot cards do not have inbuilt magical powers placed in them by the manufacturers. What they do possess, again like the Runes, is the ability to awaken the latent powers of sensory perception in their user, provided he or she allows their archetypal symbols to enter and fertilize the unconscious. The symbols on each Tarot card become the foci for the reader to turn inward and tap the psychism which we all, to a lesser or greater extent, have within ourselves.

The Runes have the same power to provide the Runecaster with the chance to unleash his or her inner psychic awareness. They can become a focusing medium used by the Runecaster to relate to the primordial images which lie behind every Rune and which have their spiritual roots in the pagan belief system. These archetypal symbols or images are the elemental spirits which the ancient Rune Masters accepted as the secret force contained within each Rune. An archetypal image in modern psychological terms is a concept or symbol of ancient origin that is so potent that it has become deeply embedded in the collective unconscious of the human race. We each shared common aspirations and fears in the past and still do so today. One common shared experience is the sensation of flying, which is recorded in the dreams of millions of people. Through the mass media and popular forms of entertainment we all share identifiable archetypal images in the form of the hero. In our modern society the hero figure may be merely the latest pop superstar, world-record-breaking athlete or Hollywood movie idol, but his influence on the group mind of the human race is no less powerful than the mythic symbolism of the pagan gods.

Each runic character in the magical alphabet used by the ancient wise ones has an archetypal image, symbolism and meanings on both a material and spiritual level. The ancient people who originated the meanings of the Runes as an oracle were realists. They lived in an environment which was harsh by modern standards (at least, by modern standards in the affluent West), but it would be wrong to regard them as primitives in the sense that word is most frequently used today. They were certainly not undeveloped or uncultured, but enjoyed a highly organized, relatively stable and socially advanced way of life. It would be wrong to make direct comparisons between the average lifestyle in pagan times and our modern society if only because of the immense technological advances we have made since the end of the Second World War. On the other hand, while the inhabitants of pagan Europe had to survive attacks by wild animals, crop failure and raids by other tribes, they were at least spared muggings, slow poisoning from pollution, urban terrorism, stress-related killer diseases and the imminent threat of global nuclear destruction. In our blind urge to worship at the altar of the new god of technological progress we are sometimes guilty of a narrow-minded vision of the modern world. After all, is it really 'progress' to move from a bow and arrow which kills a few people to modern nuclear weapons capable of vaporizing millions?

The realistic approach to life in the late Iron Age and early medieval period was reflected in the meaning and symbolism of the Runes, which deal with material matters. Just as today the average person-in-the-street is not overpreoccupied with spirituality, apart from rare participation in the rituals of the present state religion, so even in pagan times there were people who were more interested in the material rather than the spiritual side of life. Having said that, it is probable that spiritual awareness was far more widespread in pagan societies than it is today. When the average person consulted a Rune Master, his primary interest was in material matters relating to his daily life. Naturally the Rune Master obliged, but he was well aware that spiritual and material concerns cannot be separated even by disbelief in the reality of existence of that which is beyond the reach of our normal physical senses.

It was the teachings of Christianity as interpreted by the medieval Church that led to the dichotomy between spirit and matter. In their extremist reaction to what the early Christians regarded as pagan hedonism and rampant materialism, the medieval Church rejected the natural world as a sinful illusion. Some of the heretical Christian sects even went so far as to condemn the world as the false creation of the Devil. Although these heretical demonists were persecuted by the Church, their doctrines infiltrated medieval Christian theology. It was combined with the new scientific ideas formulated in the Age of Reason to form the philosophical straitjacket which has imprisoned our modern scientific and religious disciplines. The Church's teaching that the natural world is a dangerous chimera and that humanity's ultimate destiny lies in heaven after death is mirrored by the claims of scientists that the material world is the only reality and belief in any form of spiritual existence is a primitive superstition. These two conflicting views, which are both incorrect, are slowly being challenged by critics from both fields of study who realize, as did the ancient pagans, that spirit and matter are indivisible.

Superficially the magico-spiritual belief system of paganism may appear barbaric, primitive or atavistic when judged by our modern values. The image of pagan religion has been forced upon us by centuries of subtle conditioning. This brainwashing is still inherent within our education system, which teaches our children falsehoods about history. It colours the view of the outside world we receive each morning through the newspapers or the television news. The pagans of the past were not the victims of any gross manipulation of reality. Unlike ourselves, they were not conditioned by the disciples of false religious doctrines or exposed to the materialism of scientists who regard the universe as a gigantic clockwork mechanism or the accidental byproduct of a cosmic big bang.

When casting the Runes the person in charge of the operation was well aware of the unity of spirit and matter. The Runecaster had an holistic outlook on life which, in accordance with pagan beliefs, accepted that all life forms on this planet were connected in a physical and spiritual unity. One of the keystones of shamanism is the oneness of all creation. In the oldest of the creation myths it is stated that in the distant past there existed a paradisical state when humankind and the animals spoke the same language. Shamanistic traditions tell of a time known as the Great Separation when this unity was broken and the line of communication between the material world (the Middle Earth of Nordic and Teutonic mythology) and the Otherworld was severed.

The ancient pagan religions teach us how, albeit briefly, these links can be reforged and the spiritual and material once again joined as one.

In any approach to the practical aspect of runic divination the ultimate unity of spirit and matter must be considered even when interpreting the Runes from a purely material viewpoint. In our modern desecralized and nihilistic culture the idea that spirituality and materialism are reflections of each other is an alien one. Any serious study of the Runes must accept their role as an aid to understanding the cosmic pattern which gives form to the world of matter. The Runecaster regarded himself or herself as the agent of higher forces, with the divine task of interpreting the omens sent from the gods which made sense of the web of circumstances weaved by the Wyrd or the power of Fate. The Runes, or any other form of divinatory tool, should not be dismissed as a mere fortune-telling game or amusing pastime. When we deal with the Rune system we are contacting potent elemental forces which we can regard either as spiritual entities or as archetypal symbols. Either way, they have tremendous power when they interact with our psyches. By the ritual act of casting the Runes we are using them as foci for an inward journey into the depths of our own subconscious, and who knows what lurks therein? The magical images we see when we cast the Runes are just as 'real' as an aspect of reality experienced in the outer world of consciousness.

It is therefore essential that casting the Runes should be done with a serious intent, with full knowledge of the consequences, and not as a light-hearted game or something for amusement. The apprentice Runecaster should try to adopt the same attitude as the ancient Rune Masters. They spent many years, often in total isolation, learning the secrets of the Runes. In our modern society it is not possible for most people to devote such a considerable amount of time and effort to the study of any subject. However, there are several ways in which the dedicated seeker can prepare himself for Runecasting which do not involve antisocial behaviour likely to draw adverse comment from friends and relatives.

The first essential to studying the Runes is to learn their meanings, both spiritual and material. Written documentation relating to the use of the Runes is rare. The one major source of information on the symbolism of each Rune letter is *The Anglo-Saxon Rune Poem*. The first available translation of this poem into modern English dates from the early eighteenth century, but the original is believed to be medieval. Some experts have dated the original to as early as the eighth century CE but others think it dates from the eleventh century. The

monks who translated the original from Old English into Latin may
have altered its pagan content. There are certainly references and
allusions in the poem which show overt Christian influence. In the
version of *The Anglo-Saxon Rune Poem* presented here we have
attempted to expurgate the Christian influences and repaganized it in
accordance with the theme of its earliest rendition. We have also rendered it, as far as is possible without losing the original meaning, into
modern English.

First, we give the poem in its entirety and then we examine each
verse as it relates to individual Rune letters. It will soon become
apparent that, as in the major arcana of the Tarot, each letter of the
runic alphabet is a representation of the stages passed through by the
Fool (the spiritual seeker) in his or her quest to discover the meaning of
life. The ultimate truth grasped by the seeker is represented in the
Tarot as the major arcana card called 'The World'. In medieval Christian legends it is the Holy Grail, in Celtic pagan symbolism it is the
Cauldron of Inspiration belonging to the goddess Ceridwen, and in
Norse myths it is represented by the Odal Rune.

> Wealth is a consolation to everyone
> but he must share it who hopes to cast
> his lot for judgement before the gods.

> The wild ox is bold with horns ascending high
> a fierce fighter who stamps the moors.

> The thorn is very sharp and can hurt if
> gripped by anyone who comes to rest among them.

> The mouth is the origin of all speech
> it supports wisdom, brings comfort
> to the wise and blesses everyone.

> Riding a horse for a hero
> while inside the hall is soft
> It is more strenuous when astride a
> great horse riding the mile paths.

> The torch is the living flame
> pale and bright
> it burns most where noble folk
> are settled within.

> A gift to others is an ornament
> displaying wealth and to every outcast
> without any other is substance and honour.

Joy is for one who knows little sorrow
without sorrow they will have increase
and blessings.

Hail is the whitest of grains
it sweeps from the sky
is whirled by the wind
and turns to water.

Need is narrow on the breast
but can often be a help
if attended to early.

Ice is cold and slippery
it glistens bright as glass like a gem
the field covered with frost
is beautiful to see.

The season is the hope of everyone
when the gods allow the earth to
give her bright increase to rich and poor.

The yew is outwardly a smooth tree
hard and fast in the earth
a shepherd of fire
a pleasure on the land.

A lively tune means play and laughter
when warriors sit in the hall together
merry and joyful.

Sedge grows in the fen
flourishing in the water
burning the blood of everyone
who touches it.

The sun to seafarers is always confidence
when they ferry across the fishes' bath
until the seahorse brings them to land.

Tyr is a token which has the confidence of nobles
it is ever moving and in the darkness
of the night never rests.

The birch is fruitless
but has twigs without increase
is beautiful in its branches
and is laden with leaves
heavy in the air.

The horse is the joy of nobles
where heroes wealthy on their horses speak
to the restless they are a comfort.

Folk in their happiness
are dear to their kindred
and yet must everyone
depart from each other
because the gods will commit
their bodies to the earth.

Water to land folk seems tedious
if they venture forth
in an unsteady boat
the sea waves whirl them
and the seahorses do not heed
the bridle.

Ing was first seen
among the Eastern folk
departing over the waves
with his wagon
Thus the warriors named him.

Day is the gods' messenger
the light of the gods means
happiness and consolation
to rich and poor.

Home is beloved of everyone
if he prospers there in peace
and enjoys a frequent harvest.

The above poem does not make much sense in its form as rendered
above. However, when each verse is seen to relate to an individual Rune,
then more can be made of its meaning. Contained within each verse are
symbolic allusions to the Runes and these we examine next. The twenty-
four Runes which we use in this book are divided up for practical purposes into three groups of eight. These groups are known as *Aetts*, which
is an Old Norse word meaning family, tribe or clan. Each Aett is traditionally ruled by a different god from the Scandinavian pantheon. As we
progress through the twenty-four Runes the reader will see that each has
a specific magical image drawn from either Middle Earth or the realm of
the gods. Others have a more abstract symbolism associated with them.
In our description of the Runes the magico-spiritual pattern will slowly
develop and become more evident as we progress towards the mystical
twenty-fifth Rune known as the Wyrd.

THE RUNIC ORACLE

Frey's Aett

FEOH

Frey

Wealth is a consolation to everyone
but he must share it who hopes to cast his lot for
judgement before the gods.

DIVINATION MEANING
Upright: Money, success and great wealth
Reversed: Bankruptcy, loss of personal esteem

This Rune is sacred to the Norse god of fertility, Frey. Literally translated, the word Frey means 'Lord' and in some versions of the poem the last line reads 'his lot for judgement before the Lord'. In Norse myth Frey was the phallic god of peace, happiness and plenty. No sacrifices were made to Frey, for it was considered morally reprehensible to shed blood in his worship. No weapons could be carried into his temples because war was the antithesis of his message for humankind. Frey belongs to the Nordic pantheon of elder gods known as the Vanir. They were worshipped as deities of fertility, wisdom, love and peace by the pre-Iron Age Scandinavian people.

The Feoh Rune denotes phallic power expressed through the symbol of cattle, which were a sign of wealth among the Indo-European tribes. The esoteric message hidden in this verse of the poem and associated with the Rune is that money or material possessions should not be regarded as a means to an end. In our modern consumer society the pursuit of happiness through the acquisition of material objects has become a sickness. Frequently this happiness is exposed as a sham because gross materialism cannot provide psychological security, even if briefly it produces physical comfort. If money is not to become a burden it must be shared with those less fortunate, otherwise the Wyrd will not be easily disposed towards the miserly user in the afterlife. The last line may refer to the user of wealth casting the Runes before Frey and receiving bad omens. Alternatively it may refer to the judgement of the gods on the spirit of the deceased when he or she passes to the Otherworld.

On a spiritual level, the Feoh Rune teaches us that the treasures of the spirit, the secret teachings within all genuine religious systems, should not be kept hidden by an esoteric elite or a closed priesthood but taught openly to those who thirst for knowledge. All too often in the past the truth has been obscured or withheld deliberately by those few who have gained authority within a religious power structure. They have jealously guarded the secrets, often changing their original meaning to confuse the masses or to keep them enslaved by perpetual ignorance. The truth has been distorted for their own political purposes and they have exterminated those who sought to rediscover the Ancient Wisdom in its original pure state. The Feoh Rune is a symbol of the materialistic person who has reached a certain stage in his ordinary life when the glittering prizes offered by the society in which he lives no longer have any meaning. It is then that he begins to search for higher ideals and to take his first faltering steps on the woodland path of the sacred quest.

UR

Power

The wild ox is bold with horns ascending high
a fierce fighter who stamps the moors.

DIVINATION MEANING
Upright: Good fortune and advancement in a career
Reversed: Missed opportunities, negative influences, bad luck and minor illnesses

The wild ox mentioned in this verse is a symbol of raw elemental power, strength and virility. On a mundane level, the Ur Rune is symbolic of the personal aggrandisement of the querant and the motivating force in his material journey round the wheel of life. On a spiritual level, it is a Rune symbolic of individuality and the quest by the self for personal enlightenment outside the normal channels open to the masses.

Esoterically, horns have always been a very important spiritual symbol. They signify sacredness, divine origin and spiritual as opposed to temporal power. In the Judeo-Christian Bible we read of 'the horns of the altar', which were ritual attachments at the four corners of the altar stone indicating that divinity was present. Medieval artists frequently depicted famous heroes or biblical characters sprouting horns. This is not an indication of their devilish nature but a sign that they are in direct communication with divine forces. In some representations of Odin he is depicted with horns, and we have already seen his links with Herne the Hunter and the horned stag god Cernunnos.

In the pagan Old Religion horns represented life energy and sexuality. The various horned gods of pagan mythology were regarded as the messengers between the material world or Middle Earth and the realm of the gods. The shaman who wore the antlers of a stag, symbolizing the horned god, was his earthly representative communicating between the spirit world and the tribe. Horns are a symbol of regeneration and growth both physically and spiritually. The sigil can be both masculine and feminine. Outwardly the horn is the male's erect penis prepared to pour forth the life-giving semen. Inwardly the horn is hollow and resembles the female vagina, which is the receptacle of the life force and transforms it by the act of physical creation within the womb.

In Nordic religious rites the wild ox was often the animal chosen for sacrifice to the gods. Its death carried with it the meaning of self-sacrifice leading to advancement. Therefore the Ur Rune represents the ability of the awakened individual (the person who has risen from the zombie-like sleep of material existence) to assert himself in life and make good use of the power of the Wyrd or Fate. This individual is the seeker stepping out without fear on to the spiritual path to face the challenges and obstacles the gods will place before him.

THORN

Thor

The thorn is very sharp and can hurt if gripped by anyone who comes to rest among them.

DIVINATION MEANING
Upright: Protection. An important decision to be made. Good news from afar
Reversed: A hasty decision will be made. Bad news

In direct contrast to the power and strength of the auroch or wild ox of the previous verse, we have the thorn. Although tiny in comparison, it can still cause extreme discomfort, especially if encountered in great numbers. The thorn represents the small trials in life which have to be overcome by the seeker of spiritual truth. The prick of one thorn may not be too serious but the person who falls into a thorn bush may be torn quite badly.

In themselves these minor tests of endurance and character may not appear to be too important but they are essential experiences in relation to the quest. If we cannot overcome and control the petty irritations met on the wheel of life we will never be able to reach the supreme goal of spiritual self-knowledge and illumination.

In some versions of the poem this Rune's title is translated as 'giant' or 'demon', but this is probably a later Christian interpretation when the runic alphabet was becoming transformed into a diabolical device.

Most early writers equate Thorn with the thunder god Thor, who is associated with feats of superhuman endurance. On the spiritual level, the Thorn Rune is symbolic of the early tests which the seeker has to pass through on the woodland path. If he or she falls at this point having failed the minor tests, then the trees will close in hiding the object of the quest.

OS

Odin

The mouth is the origin of all speech
it supports wisdom, brings comfort to the wise and
blesses everyone.

DIVINATION MEANING
Upright: Wisdom or good counsel given by an elderly
person. Inheritances. Communication
Reversed: An elderly person causes trouble. Rumours
and untruths. Bad advice from someone who means
harm

The Os Rune is generally associated with the concept of the supreme being in Norse and Teutonic mythology. In general terms the supreme being during the later historical period when the runic correspondences were under formulation was Odin, as his title of Allfather suggests. He was the cosmic masculine principle of the life force which permeates the universe and gives manifestation to Middle Earth. In the valid context of Jungian psychology, Odin is the old wise man, the archetypal magician and shaman. The original name of the Os Rune was *Ansuz* which translated means 'Prince of Asgard and Lord of Valhalla', titles employed to describe Odin.

As we have seen, the Romans who discovered the worship of Odin/Woden among the Germanic tribes equated the hooded god with their deity Mercury, who was the messenger of the Gods. This Rune refers to the art of oral communication used by the ancient priesthood to pass on the teachings and philosophy of the Ancient Wisdom. The Celtic Druids trained for twenty years before they were accepted as initiates of the bardic brotherhood. Their training involved the memorization of lengthy poems containing esoteric knowledge. It seems probable that the Rune Masters, shamans and priests of the Old Faith experienced a similiar training technique. Certainly most of the runic knowledge which has survived has done so because it was encapsulated in verse. The only other information we have on the Rune system originates from the written accounts of foreign historians and biased monks.

The Os Rune teaches the seeker that in life he must speak softly and that wisdom may come from unexpected sources. It is associated with sacred songs, poetry and *galdr* or magical incantations. All these were taught by Odin, who learned them either by his self-sacrifice on the World Tree or through losing his eye to the guardian of the well of wisdom.

RAD

Wheel

Riding a horse for a hero while inside the hall is soft
It is more strenuous when astride a great horse riding the mile paths.

DIVINATION MEANING
Upright: Travel. A journey or holiday bringing happiness or an advancement in life's goals
Reversed: Delays. An unpleasant journey. A visit to sick relatives or friends in trouble

There is an element of wry if not sarcastic humour in this particular verse of *The Anglo-Saxon Rune Poem*. Its meaning suggests that those who sit in the comfort of their own homes telling tales of past adventures in faraway places or offering unwelcome advice on how others should lead their lives are not really experiencing the outside world. It is easy to be an armchair traveller or to be wise after the event, but the actuality is a little harder to deal with.

Many who set out on the spiritual path hoping to become better people in the progress and learn a little about the mysteries of the universe think they have to close themselves off from the outer world to develop inwardly. Nothing could be farther from the truth of the matter. Often it is the desire to escape from the ultra-materialism of our modern culture that acts as the trigger for embarking on the quest. This rejection of the false values of a corrupt system of morality should never be confused with the total rejection of the natural world or Middle Earth. This attitude is understandable in view of the narrow-minded philosophical viewpoint which is the foundation of our present society. However, the pagan concept was that the spiritual and the material were interlinked and if you rejected one then you could never attain the other. Only by experiencing both equally could the aspirant to the mysteries obtain any degree of mystical enlightenment.

On another level the Rad Rune has another meaning. There are some who set out on the quest believing they will gain their goal with the minimum of effort. With the revival of interest in occult (hidden) matters in recent years and the resulting easy access to previously esoteric sources of arcane knowledge, this attitude has become an increasingly common one among spiritual seekers. This minority interpret the old occult maxim 'When the pupil is ready the teacher will come' as an excuse for sitting down and waiting for the promised guru to materialize. There are no gurus in the Eastern sense of that word in paganism, although there are obviously divine or semi-divine figures, such as Odin or Merlin, who take on the role of a spiritual guide to the seeker. At unexpected moments these guides will pop up in the life of the seeker, cunningly disguised in human form, to offer advice and knowledge. However, the seeker must live up to that name and search in the material world for truth. The Rad Rune teaches us that the seeker should not be afraid to travel the highways and byways of the outside world in order to gain experience, even though the path will often lead back to his or her starting point. Life is the great initiation and the Wyrd (Fate) is the greatest initiator we can find.

CEN

Fire

The torch is the living flame
pale and bright
it burns most where noble folk are settled within.

DIVINATION MEANING
Upright: Guidance from people of high social standing. Illumination
Reversed: Loss of social prestige and/or valuable possessions

A torch, flame or lantern is a symbolic representation of enlightenment in many religions. In the distant past a protective ring of burning torches set around the perimeter of an encampment was a practical defence against wild animals or a surprise attack by human enemies. In Norse mythology fire is one of the twin primal energies which created and then sustained the universe. It symbolizes the masculine creative force which flows freely through Middle Earth, renewing and destroying everything in its path.

The claim in the verse that the flame of the torch will burn brightest in the proximity of noble folk is a cryptic comment. It may refer to the fact that only a large settlement, housing many aristocrats or royalty, would have many torches aflame. Spiritually, the noble folk may be a code for initiates of the mysteries whose inner light shines to guide the seeker along the woodland path. Alternatively there may be some link here with the funeral pyres of Viking chiefs. As longships were expensive items in Norse society, the cremation ceremony during which the ship was set alight was reserved only for special members of the clan. On a purely spiritual level (literally), the 'noble folk' of the verse could be a euphemism for the spirits of the dead. In popular folklore the phenomena known variously as corpse candles, will-o'-the-wisps or jack-o'-lanterns seen near Christian graveyards or ancient pagan burial mounds and believed to be spirits wandering abroad is still strong. No doubt such folk beliefs were common to our Scandinavian and Saxon ancestors.

The Cen Rune teaches the seeker that as well as progressing individually on the spiritual path he should allow his inner light or spirit glow to shine out to illuminate the lives of others who are still in the darkness of ignorance.

GYFU

Gift

A gift to other is an ornament displaying wealth and to every outcast without any other is substance and honour.

DIVINATION MEANING
Upright: A gift indicating shared love and the cementing of a relationship
Reversed: Separation. The end of a friendship or love affair. Sadness caused by those close to the querant

This is a difficult verse to interpret without first understanding that in the tribal society which practised Runecraft the giving of gifts had a special significance lost to us today. The giving of a gift placed a deep responsibility on both the giver and the receiver and was an act heavy with concealed symbolism. A person was judged socially by the number of gifts he or she bestowed on those less worthy. From a religious angle the term 'a gift for the gods' was an euphemism for a sacrifice offered in the temple to the deity of the sacrificer's choice. This sacrifice was usually a small animal but it could also be a human being. This aspect of paganism is impossible to defend morally. Some writers have claimed that sacrifice was a debased practice which only appeared when paganism had reached a degenerate stage in its development. Unfortunately, the historical evidence suggests otherwise, that blood sacrifice was a universal religious practice in pagan times.

In ceremonies to Odin, prisoners-of-war or criminals found guilty of capital offences were sentenced to die ritually. The accepted method of execution was strangulation by a leather thong. This seems to be a very ancient form of ritual killing, as can be seen from the evidence provided by the discovery of the mummified Iron Age corpses preserved in the Danish peat bogs. The ritual executions using a leather noose may possibly have been a perverted symbolic rite connected with the period the hooded god spent hanging on the sacred World Tree, especially as after their death the bodies of sacrificial victims were hung from trees near pagan shrines.

Again, the Gyfu is a Rune of self-sacrifice which teaches that the spiritual seeker always has a price to pay for advancement on the path to self-awareness and occult knowledge.

Joy is for one who knows little sorrow
without sorrow they will have increase and blessings.

DIVINATION MEANING
Upright: Happiness. The transformation of life for the better
Reversed: Unhappiness. The loss of affection from loved ones

On the spiritual level the inner meaning of the Wyn Rune is contained in the first line. This indicates the hard life endured by most people in Europe at the time when the runic alphabet was in common use. Real joy and happiness were highlights in a life which was a constant struggle against a generally hostile environment. The hard toil of the average farm worker was, of course, enlivened by celebrations which were usually of a religious nature or coincided with major events in the agricultural year. These were uninhibited celebrations involving the worship of the life force in its myriad manifestations. In the translation of the verse from *The Anglo-Saxon Rune Poem*, the condition or experience of limitless joy is presented as a utopian dream which, if ever achieved, will lead to an ideal society where peace and plenty will be abundant.

The Wyn Rune teaches the spiritual seeker that happiness arises out of any situation from which sorrow is absent. We should learn to appreciate those moments of happiness which punctuate what may seem to be long periods of misery. It is very easy when we look around at the world today to become depressed by the tragedies of everyday existence. This Rune offers the promise that present trends can be reversed and people can lead lives which are enriching and happy. The tendency to give in to pessimism is both negative and self-destructive. Even at the very depths of unhappiness there are opportunities to rise above the depression. Often unhappiness is self-inflicted, and if we realize this limitation and understand that on the wheel of life we are being tested by the power of the Wyrd, then we can learn to adopt a more positive attitude to the trials and tribulations of daily living.

With the Wyn Rune we end our journey through Frey's Aett, which represents the first steps of the aspirant towards the ultimate goal. Having decided to set out on the sacred quest, the first eight Runes offer the seeker pointers to the rest of his or her symbolic inner journey. Having reached this stage, the seeker is now ready to leave the comforts of the material world represented as the home in Frey's Aett and encounter the forces of nature in their own realm.

5

The first eight Runes of Frey's Aett deal on a superficial level with the material life of the spiritual seeker. Their symbols include wealth, strength, protection, wisdom, travel, illumination, gifts and joy. Each is associated on a mundane level with the comforts of the home, although obviously they also have inner interpretations. The second Aett of eight Runes takes us beyond the great hall where the warriors sit and drink mead and poets recount the adventures of the gods and heroes. We now venture into the outside world ruled by the elemental forces of nature personified as divine beings by the pagans.

Haegl's Aett

HAGEL

Air

Hail is the whitest of grains
it sweeps from the sky
is whirled by the wind and turns to water.

DIVINATION MEANING
Upright: Sickness. A delay in plans because the Wyrd is not working for the querant
Reversed: Disasters caused by natural forces. Delays created by forces beyond human control

In this verse of *The Anglo-Saxon Rune Poem* hail represents the power of the Wyrd or Fate to control the destiny of the human race. On a cold winter or spring day a sudden shower of hail may suddenly drop from a blue sky without warning. Likewise, the forces of the Wyrd may suddenly change plans or cause delays in projects or life purposes which have been proceeding smoothly.

The victims of the Wyrd's capricious influence may feel they are being swept along by forces which they cannot control. But in the sunshine which follows stormy weather the hail as it melts is transformed into water. This signifies that the restrictions of the Wyrd will vanish but that they must be endured for a reason which may not be clear to the seeker at the time. We can never hope to control the power of the Wyrd, but we can learn to understand its movements and anticipate its flow so that we can work with it and not against it. Even the Runes as a divinatory device can only *indicate* or advise the path we should take. The shaman or magician who seeks to control the elemental forces is an agent of the Wyrd in the same way as any ordinary person. The exception is that he has more knowledge of the Wyrd's workings and can act accordingly.

The Haegl Rune is called the Rune of Air. This is because the power of the Wyrd flows like the wind. One moment it can be a breeze and the next it is a gale. In recognizing the forces of destiny which shape our lives and give them meaning, the seeker of truth perceives the eternal cycle of death and rebirth which sustains the cosmos. Through this mystical experience the seeker becomes aware of the divine pattern behind reality and his or her role as a microcosmic entity within the greater macrocosmos.

NYD

Necessity

Need is narrow on the breast but can often be a help if attended to early.

DIVINATION MEANING
Upright: Greed must be guarded against. Caution is recommended if all plans are to succeed
Reversed: Do not act rashly. Less haste more speed. A quick judgement leads to disaster

The key words ruling the Nyd Rune are *need, necessity* and *compulsion*. This verse in the poem warns the querant or the seeker that material desires can be self-destructive. The present social system which has developed since the Industrial Revolution is based on state or private capitalism (whatever political label it uses to describe itself) and the acquisition of material objects. The Nyd Rune teaches us that material possessions should not be sought after to the point of obsession. It would be wrong totally to reject the comforts offered by a materialistically inclined lifestyle but we should keep a balanced view of our needs. All too often our materialistic culture offers us a dream paradise of consumer delights to strive after. If we examine the reasons for this policy we will see that it has more to do with the survival of the work ethic and the continuance of the established political power structure than it has about the wellbeing of the enslaved and docile consumer.

If the seeker can cast off the shackles of materialism he can recognize that there is a spiritual dimension to the material world. This Rune verse suggests that the consumer will reach a point in his or her life where the desire for material pleasure will act as the trigger which reverses the life direction towards the spiritual. The Nyd Rune offers us a first glimpse of the magical Otherworld which co-exists with the physical plane, but which, because of our totally materialistic outlook, is only experienced when we free ourselves from the self-imposed constraints of desire.

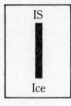

IS

Ice

Ice is cold and slippery
it glistens bright as glass like a gem
the field covered with frost is beautiful to see.

DIVINATION MEANING
Upright: An obstacle to progress. The emotional cooling of a relationship
Reversed: Disagreements with close friends or relatives

In the Norse creation myth ice is the inert primal force eternally in conflict with fire. Through this cosmic struggle the universe was created and remains stable. Ice is frozen water, and spiritually the Isa Rune signifies the transformation of the seeker from one stage of development to another.

The first line of the verse emphasizes the negative attributes of ice. In the next line we see that while ice can be treacherous it also 'glistens bright as glass like a gem'. The concluding lines suggest that the cosmic force of ice is a double-edged power, both positive and negative.

It would be incorrect to interpret the cosmic conflict between the primal forces of ice and fire as a battle between good and evil as in the orthodox Christian world view. Fire and ice have to oppose each other, for in their meeting point is created universal harmony. It is for this reason that the negative aspects of the Isa Rune are harmonized by a vision of the beauty of nature in her winter glory.

GER

Earth

The season is the hope of everyone
when the gods allow the earth to
give her bright increase to rich and poor.

DIVINATION MEANING
Upright: A period of waiting. A warning not to speak ill of others or judge them before all the facts are known
Reversed: Problems with the law. Harsh words spoken rashly which are regretted

The Ger Rune represents growth, fertility, rebirth and regeneration. The season mentioned in the first line of the verse is the end of summer, the growing period of the year, when the harvest is gathered in. In some versions of *The Anglo-Saxon Rune Poem* the words 'the gods' are replaced by 'Heaven's king' or 'The High King'. These words mean either Frey, the male god of fertility, whose major festival was celebrated at harvest time, or the ruler of the tribe, who was the gods' representative on Middle Earth. This Rune is also sacred to Nerthus, the Great Earth Mother Goddess, who was widely worshipped in Northern Europe in the Bronze and Iron Ages.

Spiritually, the Ger Rune signifies the end of a dark cycle in the self-awareness of the seeker/querant and the beginning of a more positive stage. Events which occur under this Rune are slow to develop, as the time period indicated in its divinatory meaning suggests. The Rune symbolizes the ending of a cycle or a stage of the journey of the quest and the beginning of another which will take the seeker farther towards the goal.

On another level of understanding this Runic letter is associated with the natural law of the universe. This should not be confused with the transitory laws made by humankind or even with the standards of morality created by historical social groups. This Rune teaches us that if we sow our seed correctly then we will reap a just harvest in accordance with cosmic laws. The esoteric meaning of the Ger Rune is that everything moves in cycles and that our modern linear concept of time flowing from one point to another in a straight line is a false one. Our present culture has an egocentric concept of progress from the Stone Age to our modern technological age, but the Ger Rune suggests that this is an illusion based on a totally misunderstood notion about the workings of the cosmic pattern.

The yew is outwardly a smooth tree
hard and fast in the earth
a shepherd of fire
a pleasure on the land

DIVINATION MEANING
Upright: Death. Delays. News of a friend or enemy from the past
Reversed: Death. A return to old problems. An illusory nostalgia for the past

The title of the Eoh Rune has a sinister connotation, but its meaning is softened if you take a realistic approach to the end of life and see it as a normal process which we must all eventually participate in. Once the idea that matter and spirit are one is accepted, then the act of dying ceases to be such a threat. Obviously we all worry about the manner of our death; it would be nice if we could all die at an old age in our sleep in our own bed surrounded by friends and relatives. The Wyrd dictates otherwise. We are all manifestations of the life force and it is to it that we return after death. All religious belief systems have created an afterlife which represents the society in which its worshippers have lived on Middle Earth taken to its highest ideal. The Northern European people were no exception, and Valhalla is conceived of as a huge hall where a great fire blazes eternally and the mead cups never run dry. Such fairy tales are symbolic representations of the afterlife state and should not be ridiculed, for they are probably valid images which will condition the spirit to the reality of existence after physical death.

The verse in *The Anglo-Saxon Rune Poem* takes as its symbolic centrepoint or focus the yew tree. In popular folklore and pagan belief the yew is traditionally the tree of the dead. This is confirmed by the fact that copses of yews are frequently found in old churchyards. On a practical level, they also offered a useful protection to the church from winter storms. In Nordic mythology the yew is the tree sacred to Odin in his guise as Lord of the Wild Hunt riding the night sky gathering up the souls of the dead. Although the yew in folk myth is the tree of death, it is also an evergreen and offers the promise that nature will be regenerated in the spring. According to another old folk belief, the wood of a yew when seasoned can be as hard as iron and last as long. It is also good for burning, and fire is a symbol of regeneration through creative destruction.

The Eoh Rune advises the seeker on the woodland path that death is nothing to fear. In the classical mysteries the candidate for initiation symbolically endured death and rebirth. Many of the old pagan gods experienced death and were then resurrected in a representation of the cycle of the seasons from winter through to summer. In Norse myth it is Baldur who dies but is mysteriously reborn to become the leader of a new order of gods after the final battle of Ragnarok. One of the most important ceremonies in the old Northern European pagan religion was celebrated in springtime with the ritual mating of human representatives of the god and goddess of fertility. In this ceremony, by the act of physical love the participants reaffirmed the power of nature to conquer even death.

PEORTH

Hearth

A lively tune means play and laughter when warriors sit in the hall together merry and joyful.

DIVINATION MEANING
Upright: Hidden knowledge. Unexpected gains from a mysterious source. A person who acts as a spiritual guide in the querant's life
Reversed: Secrets from the past will be revealed. A skeleton in the cupboard exposed to public view

Translations of the meaning of the Peorth Rune vary considerably. For our purpose we have accepted the standard association indicated in *The Anglo-Saxon Rune Poem* by the reference to a musical tune and entertainment. It is well known that the sacred can be appreciated or experienced through the medium of song and dance. In medieval society the jester or fool was an important figure at social gatherings. Outwardly he would be a clown, but the mask of the jester concealed the bard or wise man (the *wita*) whose music and rhyme were a code for esoteric knowledge. The role of the bard in Celtic culture is legendary, and it is evident that in Northern Europe there were wandering shamans who took on a similiar role. These Norse bards would not only have been storytellers who related the great sagas to their spellbound audiences but also teachers of the mysteries, including Runecraft.

To the ancient German people the power of ritualized poetry was very influential in magical and spiritual practices. Sacred songs were also an important aspect of shamanic worship and the term covered everything from personal prayers to priestly invocations. The person who knew the old songs and poems was socially respected in the medieval period and was represented by the jester. It is no coincidence that the male witch in the seventeenth-century painting mentioned earlier (see p. 54) should have been wearing a jester's cap.

The Peorth Rune indicates a stage in the quest when the seeker will receive help to progress from an outsider. This person will act as a spiritual guide, pointing the seeker in the correct direction at a crucial stage in his or her development. It would be naive to think that this guide will appear in one of the traditional guises associated with spiritual guides of the pagan past such as Odin, Merlin or even Gandalf. Just as the jester's mask hides the wise man, so the spirit guide and the advice it gives may not be easy to recognize at first. Symbolically, the seeker is also the Fool who is travelling along the path of life towards the goal of adepthood. The Peorth Rune illustrates that not everything is as it seems and it would be wrong to take things solely at face value.

EOLH

Protection

Sedge grows in the fen
flourishing in the water
burning the blood of everyone who touches it.

DIVINATION MEANING
Upright: Protection. The warding-off of negative
influences. A new career begins
Reversed: Danger from outsiders. People who mis-
lead must be avoided. Material loss which will never
be regained

The Eolh Rune is a symbolic representation of the many dangers
inherent in the quest. These are the 'temptations' which lurk on either
side of the woodland path and by their presence divert the seeker's
attention from the truth. It is difficult for the seeker to balance the
demands of the inner and outer world. A balance must be achieved, for
the way of the hermit is not one which we can afford to follow within
the confines of our modern social system. Such an approach to the
spiritual life can lead to the rejection of the natural world, which is at
odds with the aims of development within a pagan belief system. Both
the material and the spiritual should be harmonized so that the best of
both approaches can be used to enrich life.

This Rune shape has been compared with an old German gesture to
ward off evil spirits. The person being threatened held up three fingers
with the palm of the hand facing outwards towards the source of
alleged evil. This gesture of protection may also be connected with the
horned sign used in the Middle Ages as a defence against the evil eye.
To make this sign, the first and little fingers are upraised and the other
fingers folded in towards the palm. This was a secret sign used for
recognition purposes by followers of the medieval witch cult who were
traditionally worshippers of the pagan Horned God.

The esoteric message of this Rune is that the seeker will encounter
people on the path who will attempt to persuade him that he should
abandon his search. This will be accomplished either by offering
material distractions or by the promise of alternative forms of spirituality which are better than the seeker's chosen one. The shape and
meaning of this Rune denotes that the aspirant will be protected from
these distractions and will continue the quest strengthened in his or
her resolve to complete it.

The sun to seafarers is always confidence when they ferry across the fishes' bath until the seahorse brings them to land.

DIVINATION MEANING
Upright: Health. The life force. Guidance in life
Reversed: A warning to monitor health matters. Over-exertion could be dangerous to wellbeing

In the verse relating to the Sigil Rune the sun is depicted as a guiding light to seafarers. Two powerful pagan symbols are linked together in this verse – the sun and the sea – and not without a purpose. Symbolically, the sun represents the life force, but in Germanic mythology the sun was regarded as feminine. Even today in some parts of Germany the sun is known as Frau Sonne, indicating its female nature. Both the sun and the sea are therefore symbols of the feminine principle to the Northern European peoples, although in the later patriarchal period gods like Baldur were associated with the solar myth.

In relation to the quest, the Sigil Rune signifies the higher self of the seeker which, if contacted, can guide us across the sea of experience. The symbolism of the sun and the sea represents the union between heaven and earth, matter and spirit, male and female. It is the mystical conjunction of opposites which is the key to the true spiritual transformation of the individual.

With the Sigil Rune we reach the end of our symbolic journey through Haegl's Aett which represent the elemental forces of nature. We must now take our first tentative steps through the Runic symbols of Tyr's Aett which will lead us ultimately to our spiritual goal.

Tyr's Aett

Tyr is a token which has the confidence of nobles
It is ever moving and in the darkness of the night never rests.

DIVINATION MEANING
Upright: A passionate love affair which will be long lasting. Emotional happiness
Reversed: Frustrated love. Marital unhappiness. Emotional problems

In Norse pagan religion Tyr or Tiw is the god of war. He is one of the principle deities of the family of divine beings known as the Aesir. The other important deities are Odin Allfather, the goddess of love Frigga and the thunder god Thor. Tyr gave his name to Tuesday and was equated by the Romans with their god of war Mars. When it is close to earth the red planet Mars is one of the brightest objects in the sky, and, of course, as it rises and sets every night, it 'never rests'.

This Rune represents the goal which the traveller on the sacred quest is seeking, i.e. spiritual enlightenment. The closer he or she gets towards it the farther away it seems to recede, just like the planet Mars, which appears from our earthly vantage point to move quickly across the night sky between its rising and setting points.

Another meaning of this runic letter is courage and tenacity. In the Northern myths it is Tyr who elects to bind the dreaded Fenris Wolf when it threatens the cosmic order. Only by allowing the wolf to hold his hand in its mouth can Tyr persuade it to be chained. As soon as the chains are tightened the Fenris Wolf bites off the hand that fooled him. Tyr sacrificed his hand that the cosmic order should be preserved. This teaches the seeker that courage is needed to tread the spiritual path. Although Tyr is a god of warfare, he represents the destructive power of the male life principle harnessed for positive and creative ends.

BEORC

Birch

The birch is fruitless
but has twigs without increase
is beautiful in its branches
and is laden with leaves
heavy in the air.

DIVINATION MEANING
Upright: New beginnings, birth, growth, marriage
Reversed: Stagnation, separation, divorce

In folklore the birch tree is featured in fertility rites and is sacred to the Great Goddess. The birch was regarded as luck because emblems or symbols representing sexuality are regarded as powerful protectors against misfortune. In many parts of Europe peasants still wear small phallic amulets to ward off bad luck. Cowrie shells, which resemble the female sex organ, have a similiar magical power to combat evil forces. Birch twigs were used in pagan rites for flagellation, which is a very ancient practice to promote fertility. In some pagan ceremonies the altar was the naked body of the priestess. In such rituals she would traditionally lie on an improvised bed of birch twigs and wild flowers. In medieval Europe the Maypole was often made from a birch tree. This again links the birch with the sexual rites of early spring to promote growth and greenery. It was at the May Day festivities that many 'greenwood marriages' were consummated. These sexual liaisons were designed to last only for the summer.

The verse of *The Anglo-Saxon Rune Poem* which describes the Beorc Rune says that although the birch has no fruit it is still a beautiful tree. This Rune again teaches the seeker that he or she should not be deluded by outside appearances. The inner reality is often quite different. This lesson is also taught in the Celtic legends in which the hero (the seeker on the spiritual path) encounters an old hag who insists he makes love to her. Overcoming his revulsion, the hero obliges and the crone is transformed into a nubile young woman who is, of course, the goddess of fertility. When the old myths became transformed into fairy tales with a patriarchal bias, it was the princess who kissed a frog which turned into a handsome prince.

The latent sexuality of the Beorc Rune also indicates to the seeker that, unlike the Christian religion, which denies the life force, salvation can be gained by the 'pleasures of the flesh'. The use of sexual energy for magical and spiritual purposes was a feature of the pagan Old Religion. In pre-Christian times it was recognized that the sex act could be the highest form of worshipping the life force. This aspect of paganism shocked the early Church which sought to eradicate sexuality from religion. By doing so it sowed the destructive seeds of sexual inhibition, phobia and repression whose bitter harvest we are reaping today in our modern society.

A little-known aspect of this Rune links it with the use of the sacred red-capped toadstool *Amanita muscaria* or fly agaric, which was utilized by North European shamans when they sought to contact the spirit world. This narcotic fungi grows especially well in birch forests.

EH

Horse

The horse is the joy of nobles
where heroes wealthy on their horses speak to the restless
they are a comfort.

DIVINATION MEANING
Upright: Travel. House removal. Change of job
Reversed: Restlessness. Frustrating journey ending in failure

In pagan Northern Europe horses were animals that were especially sacred to the gods. The Indo-European tribes who colonized North and West Europe had tamed the wild horse, and their religious myths reflect this fact. Ancient sites such as the Uffington White Horse bear witness to this fact. At Uffington in Berkshire a giant white horse of Celtic design has been carved into the white chalk of the hillside. A few miles away is a prehistoric burial mound known locally as Wayland's Smithy. We examine the legend of Weland or Wayland in Part Three (see pp. 128–9) when we explore the gods and goddesses of the Norse and Saxon pagan religion.

The horse symbol of the Eh Rune refers to the sacred horses which draw the solar wagon across the sky each day. It also refers to the horse as the steed used by the shaman to travel to the Otherworld. On a symbolic level, the Eh Rune teaches the seeker to keep control of his emotions if he wishes to make progress in life. In the previous verse of the poem the liberating power of the life force was described. In contrast, this Rune teaches that there are times when control of the emotions is required to achieve spiritual attainment.

MAN

Man

Folk in their happiness are dear to their kindred and yet must everyone depart from each other because the gods will commit their bodies to the earth.

DIVINATION MEANING
Upright: Relatives. Conflict with officialdom or the outside world which enlarges the querant's perspective on life
Reversed: Danger from hidden enemies. Self-imposed isolation from the family for reflective purposes

In this verse the position of the seeker within the family is clarified. This family can either be his or her relatives by blood or law or the greater family of the rest of humanity. Kinship was very important to the North Europeans and this concept extended beyond life into the realm of death. It was the family who built the mound or dug the grave where the dead were interred. It was the task of the family to keep the grave properly tended and to ensure that the departed did not become a 'death walker', which is the Norse term for an earthbound spirit.

This Rune suggests that a time comes when the seeker must leave the security of the family and make his or her own life in the outside world. The umbilical cord which binds the seeker to family and friends has to be cut once the first steps on the spiritual path are taken. Frequently one encounters those who have embarked on the quest who find it difficult to relate to their family or old friends. New relationships must then be forged, or if this is not possible, then the seeker must accept that the path he is walking will be a lonely one. It is not always possible to find other people of like mind who understand where you are coming from. As progress is made on the esoteric path, the seeker will find it increasingly difficult to find others who can share the unique experience of the quest.

On the final journey we make in life through the gates of death we will be alone. But as we pass through these gates from Middle Earth to the shadowy realm of the Otherworld we know that we will be greeted by the spirits of those who have gone before us.

LAGU

Water

Water to land folk seems tedious if they venture forth in an unsteady boat
the sea waves whirl them and the seahorses do not heed the bridle.

DIVINATION MEANING
Upright: Journey across water. Intuition. Psychic powers
Reversed: Confusion. Delusion. Muddled thoughts

Water is a very important esoteric symbol. According to ancient occult traditions, humanity originally came from the sea. History is littered with strange legends of lost continents submerged beneath the sea and of a mysterious Sea People who colonized the civilized world. These Sea People have been identified as Atlanteans or inhabitants of the legendary hyperborean continent of Thule which was the mythical home of the Vanir gods. According to the oldest myths known to humankind, our race was born from the womb of the Great Mother Goddess which is symbolically regarded as the sea.

The Lagu Rune suggests that the seeker could find himself out of his depth in his quest. Like the landlubber who is not used to sea travel, the seeker may feel that his or her life is out of control. He is being tossed around like a boat in a storm at sea. Such periods of delusion, self-doubt and the lack of confidence which besets even the most assured person are to be expected and are all part of the Wyrd's testing process. They must be regarded as experience-forming happenings which, instead of weakening the seeker's resolve, only make him or her more determined to proceed.

ING

Fertility

Ing was first seen among the Eastern folk departing over the waves with his wagon
Thus the warriors named him.

DIVINATION MEANING
Upright: Completion. End of a cycle. Realization of a dream
Reversed: Sterility. A dream is shattered. Disruption of life by psychic forces

Ing is a mysterious deity in Norse mythology and was allegedly first sighted travelling over the sea in a wagon by the East Danes. He seems to have been a male consort of the Earth Mother, Nerthus, although he was later identified with Frey. The Saxon kings of northeast England allegedly claimed divine descent from this god, and the royal dynasty of Sweden was known as the Inglings for the same reason. Some writers have also pointed out that *Ing* is an Old English word for 'beacon'. It is therefore possible that Ing was a solar deity.

The overall meaning of the Fertility Rune is completion. On the esoteric level, this Rune means that the querant has reached a state of harmony and balance which is the result of his or her experiences on the spiritual path. Whether this state of inner harmony is a lasting one or just a passing byproduct of the quest, only time will tell. Ultimately the goal of the quest is the identification of the seeker with the balanced powers of fire and ice that rule the universe. Only by reconciling these cosmic forces within himself can the seeker achieve true happiness.

DAEG

Dawn

Day is the gods' messenger
the light of the gods means happiness and consolation to rich and poor.

DIVINATION MEANING
Upright: Prosperity. A change of life for the better
Reversed: Restraint. Life changes leading to uncomfortable circumstances

There is a slight indication of Christian dualism in this verse of *The Anglo-Saxon Rune Poem* with its emphasis on the association of light and day with the achievement of happiness. In the Norse climate, in which the winter days were short and the nights long, the waxing power of the sun in spring was a powerful sign of joy. The climax of the sun's power at midsummer was celebrated in Scandinavia with folk dances around Maypoles and the lighting of bonfires on the hills.

Daeg is also known as the Dawn Rune, which signifies not only the moment when the life-giving sun rises above the horizon but also one of the magical times when the powers of light and darkness are equal. In pagan lore, dawn and twilight are periods of the day when the veil between this world and the next is thin. It is a time for seeing ghosts, faeries and the old gods. Although the material and spiritual worlds co-exist and there can be communication between them under normal circumstances, the average person is not aware of the realm beyond the limitations of his physical senses. At dawn and dusk there exists the opportunity for even the most rational person to experience the mystery and terror of contact with the Otherworld.

As regards the seeker on the woodland path, the Daeg Rune offers the message that he or she must seek beyond the obvious duality of night and darkness to the ultimate reality. Although light has always been associated with the positive side of spirituality, we ignore the dark side at our peril. Light and dark are opposite sides of the same reality and one cannot exist without the other to complement its existence. If we deny one, then we deny the other, and the balance of opposites which sustains the cosmic pattern is threatened. The Daeg Rune represents the true nature of the universe where light and darkness, good and evil, matter and spirit, male and female are polarized and synthesized at the same time. The life force both absorbs and transcends all the opposites which we use to describe the reality in which we move and have our being. A stage is reached in the quest where the seeker becomes aware of the true nature of the universe, and this stage is the one represented in the runic alphabet by Daeg.

ODAL

Ancestral

Home is beloved of everyone if he prospers there in peace and enjoys a frequent harvest.

DIVINATION MEANING
Upright: Ancestral influences. Property. Inheritances. News from afar
Reversed: Problems with property or inheritances. A wasted communication with someone who does not answer

The Odal Rune represents the end of the seeker's journey through the runic alphabet. It is the goal which the seeker has sought so hard for. It is the sacred grove in the centre of the forest which the traveller reaches after walking down the woodland path. In some of the classical mysteries the aspirant is led through many ordeals until he reaches an empty room which is the inner sanctum of the temple. In other versions the initiate travels through a maze and finds at its centre a mirror in which is reflected his or her image.

Such devices may seem melodramatic, but they teach a valuable lesson. The realm of the gods is within you. No matter how hard you travel down the path to seek the truth, unless you realize this fact your journey will be in vain. The truth which the spiritual seeker is looking for and will eventually find is the impulse which made him or her set out on the quest in the first place.

6

Having examined in some detail the divinatory and spiritual meanings of the runic alphabet, we can now consider their practical application as a method of divination. We will begin with the preparation of a set of Runes for personal use.

In the historical description given by Tacitus the Germanic priests and shamans used a branch of a fruit-bearing tree to make their Runes. The branches were cut into strips and then carved with the runic letters. These Runes were thrown onto a white cloth and the priest/shaman picked three, at random, one at a time, and made his pronouncements according to the symbols scored on them. It has been suggested that Runes were also carved on a number of other natural materials apart from wood. These included bone, metal and stone.

A choice of materials for making a set of Runes is therefore available to the individual. They can be made from stone, wood, metal or even pottery. Obviously metal Runes could be a little heavy to carry around and a set made from pottery far too fragile. We are left, then, with the choice of either wood or stone. If we choose wood, there are several different types which for magical or mythological purposes are deemed more suitable for making Runes than any others.

The first of these is yew. As we have seen in our examination of the Eoh Rune, it is a tree associated with death, the Otherworld and Odin as the Lord of the Wild Hunt. It is a hard wood which is very durable and therefore ideally suited for a long-lasting Rune set.

Our second choice is ash, for in Norse and Germanic myth the sacred World Tree Yggdrasil is an ash tree. It is upon this tree that Odin hung for nine days and nights in order to receive the wisdom of the Runes. The third wood is oak, which is another hard wood renowned for its durability. Oaks were worshipped by our pre-Christian ancestors as symbols of the thunder or sky god. In the Bronze Age the Northern Europeans buried their dead in oak coffins because of its religious significance.

Once the wood to be used for making the Runes has been selected, then it is comparatively simple. The best size for each Rune is rectangle measuring approximately $2 \times \frac{3}{4}$ inch. The edges can be rounded off and smoothed to provide a Rune 'stone' which is nice to handle and is suitable for casting. Runes can be carved on flat square pieces of wood but these are not so practical. The actual runic letters can be carved onto the surface of the wood with a special carving tool or a chisel. Alternatively, they can be burned into the wood with a heated piece of wire. Or you can simply paint the runic letters onto the surface of each 'stone'. Remember that in addition to the twenty-four Runes which make up the three Aetts described in chapter 5, there is a twenty-fifth Rune which is left blank. This Rune represents the force of the Wyrd, which rules the runic alphabet.

Once carved, the runic letters can be coloured in accordance with ancient tradition. In the old days the Rune Masters coloured the Runes with their own blood but today we need not be so dramatic. The traditional colours are red, signifying the life force, blue, which is the colour sacred to Odin, and yellow, which is the planetary colour of Mercury whom the Romans equated with Woden.

If you do not want to use wood for your Rune set then collect twenty-five stones or pebbles of fairly uniform shape and size. The runic letters can be painted on these in the sacred colour of your choice. A nice Rune set could be made from slate, although it tends to break easily. If you feel unable to tackle the more artistic Rune sets, then you can write the runic letters on pieces of stiff cardboard in felt pen, crayon or drawing ink. This makes a very effective runic set.

The previous paragraphs have been written with the presumption that the reader will want to make his or her own Rune set, but some of us are not artistically inclined or good with our hands. In these cases, it is possible to ask someone else to make a Rune set for you. Since interest began to grow in the Runes about eight or nine years ago there have been several attempts to produce a commercialized Rune set. There are also craftsmen available who will make a set of Runes for you for a fee. As these are individually produced they can be rather expensive but the dedicated, non-artistic Runecaster may feel that the financial outlay is worthwhile.

The artistic creation of the Runes is not really as important as the *intent* of the would-be Runecaster. It is possible to become so absorbed in the actual making of a Rune set that you lose sight of the reason why you are making it.

The intention and preparation before casting Runes are all-important, even if your efforts in the field are going to be limited to casting them for yourself or close friends. The Runes are not an amusing game, and anyone who sets out to treat them in that way is likely to have a shock. Once you start working with the Runes you are using archetypal symbols that can unlock potentialities within your psyche which you may not realize existed. Before launching on your career as a Runecaster, whether for your own personal guidance or to help others, you should consider the ethical aspects of your task.

Anyone who decides that he or she will use any form of divination which involves contact with the public must first consider the reasons why the majority of people consult what they regard as a fortune teller. It will soon become clear that many people who go to see Tarot readers or Runecasters do so because they are experiencing serious emotional, psychological or physical problems. The mere act of telephoning or writing for a consultation is, for many people, a cry for help. The role of the Runecaster in such a situation is to act as a psychiatrist, confessor, therapist, healer and spiritual guide all rolled into one. This aspect of providing divination for the general public may seem very surprising to newcomers to Runecraft. They may have the naive view that all that is required of them is to tell the eager querant how many wives/husbands/babies he or she is going to have or which business offer to accept, and then take the proffered fee. In fact, the contrast made between the Runecaster and the querant extends far beyond such trivialities in most cases. Those who are contemplating using the Runes for public divination are recommended to consider carefully whether they wish to take on the degree of moral responsibility involved.

Of course, in practice not all would-be Runecasters are interested in projecting their talents into the public arena for worldly consumption. Many people are only interested in the Runes as a form of personal guidance and self-development. We will therefore examine the practical application of casting the Runes before returning to the complex issue of their use as a public method of divining future trends.

How do you cast the Runes? First, you need a suitable surface to cast the Runes on. A dark-coloured cloth is ideal. Alternatively they can be cast on a board, a neutral-coloured tray or the top of a suitable table.

Before casting the Runes, prepare yourself mentally for the task. Select each Rune in turn and handle it, studying its shape. Turn it over in your hands. Lay the Runes out in patterns or straight rows. If you are doing the reading for another person, make sure before casting that the querant also handles the Runes so that his or her personal vibrations are picked up by the stones. It is important for the Runecaster to meditate on each of the runic letters. The best way to accomplish this is to draw the twenty-four Runes on white paper with a black pen so that they stand out from their background. They can either be meditated on singly, in groups of eight or in totality. Visualize each Rune in turn and try to imagine a scene corresponding to each symbol. For instance, with Frey's Rune, imagine cattle grazing on a moor with snow-covered hills in the distance. Similiar scenes can be conjured up to fit the symbolism of the other Runes.

Before actually casting the Runes, sit in silence for a few minutes and mentally visualize the god Odin. A description of the hooded god has already been given earlier in this book. If you feel so inclined, a short invocation addressed to the god can be recited. An example is given below.

> Odin, Lord of the Wild Hunt
> Shaman God of the North Wind
> Master of the Runes
> guide my hands and heart
> as I cast these sacred signs
> may our questions be answered
> true and right
> In the names of Frey, Haegl and Tiw
> and by the power of Fire and Ice
> So mote it be.

Opinions differ on how many Runes should be cast at any one time. Some Runecasters prefer only nine, which is the mystical number of the worlds or heavens outlined on the sacred World Tree Yggdrasil. Others say that the full amount should be cast. Whatever the number chosen, the easiest way to cast the Runes is by using a bag or pouch. Mix them up thoroughly in the bag and then cast them upon the cloth or whatever surface you have chosen to display them.

Only interpret those Runes that have fallen face upwards and disregard those whose runic letters you cannot see. Of the Runes which are facing upwards, interpret those facing away from you or the querant as being in the reversed position. Place the blank Wyrd Rune back in the pouch together with those Runes whose characters are facing downwards. Mix the Runes up again and, if you are doing the reading for someone else, ask him to pick one Rune from the bag at random. If the Rune selected by this process is not the blank one, then return it to the bag.

Obviously the Runes are more accurate if a specific question is asked of them, but some people will want to have a general view of future trends. In the following example the fall of the Runes is fairly scattered and, as the querant was not asking a specific question, they were

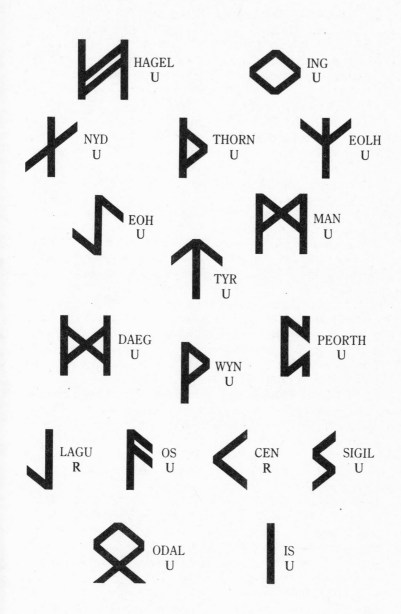

HAGEL
U

ING
U

NYD
U

THORN
U

EOLH
U

EOH
U

MAN
U

TYR
U

DAEG
U

WYN
U

PEORTH
U

LAGU
R

OS
U

CEN
R

SIGIL
U

ODAL
U

IS
U

interpreted as general portents of future events.

The querant is in her mid-thirties, self-employed, and feels that she has reached a crisis point in her life. A number of different options have been offered to her relating to the direction of her future career. Her main reason for requesting a general Rune reading was for guidance in making the right choice for her future happiness from the many opportunities presented to her.

The first two Runes to be interpreted in this reading are Nyd and Hagel. Their position suggests that any plans already made by the querant will be delayed. The reason given is because the power of the Wyrd is not working with her at the present time. In the ancient Chinese philosophy known as Taoism, which has many similiarities with the runic system, the masters of the Ancient Wisdom talk of the Flow. This is the natural rhythm of the Universe – eternal yet ever changing. Human beings either travel with the Flow or they struggle against it. We all experience periods of 'bad luck' when events seem to dominate us, when nothing goes right and everybody and everything conspires against us. Post is delayed, people around us are uncooperative for no apparent reason, plans fail and life seems to be on the verge of collapsing into chaos. At other times, everything goes smoothly and we feel confident enough to tackle any task or situation and come out on top. This is the difference between going with the Flow and fighting it. We either accept our Wyrd (Fate) or we reject it and suffer the consequences. In such a situation the Runes can offer advice on how we should proceed to identify its cause and rectify it.

The reason why the Wyrd is not at the moment working for the querant is indicated by the Nyd Rune. This indicates that she is allowing feelings of greed to dominate her life. The double meaning of this Rune is need and necessity; the two are often confused. The negative feelings experienced by the querant while seeking to sort out her problems arise from a sublimated, but no less real, desire for material progress at the expense of spiritual development. At the time that she arranged the Rune reading she was unaware of this flaw in her psyche, but it was all too apparent to those around her and has been exposed by the Runes. These negative feelings must be recognized by the querant and brought under control or the consequences for her happiness will be serious.

A period of delay is indicated by the Eoh Rune. News of a friend from the past will be useful, however, in removing this obstacle. This also links with the Ing Rune which is a portent of a realization of a dream, and the Thorn Rune which represents good news from afar. Taken together, the conjunction of three Runes means that the appearance in the querant's life of a friend from earlier years, who lives some distance from her and from whom she may have lost contact, will more than compensate for the negative effects of the delay.

The Man Rune in the layout represents a person with official status who will be an important factor in the querant's life in the near future. This contact will seem at first to be an unfortunate encounter. Events which subsequently arise will prove this judgement to be unfounded. Experiences associated with this official person will change in a very subtle way the querant's perspective of the outside world. Through the encounter with this person the querant will find inner strength of purpose and this will ultimately help her in her situation.

When we find the Eolh Rune in a reading it indicates that a new career prospect is on the horizon. This fits in with an offer already made to the querant which she has not yet decided to accept. The fact that the next runic letter is Daeg means that the offer will bring a change of lifestyle for the better; a new day is dawning. This is doubly confirmed by the next Rune being Wyn which represents happiness and a change of life for the better. Close to Wyn and Daeg is the Tyr Rune. This indicates emotional happiness which may arise from a love affair or, perhaps, considering the situation the querant finds herself in, from material security.

On a mundane level the position of the Peorth Rune in the reading is an indication that the querant will receive a gift from an unexpected or anonymous source. If we interpret this Rune on a more esoteric level it indicates that the querant will become involved with the occult mysteries. This could result from her present indecision regarding her future life, which might lead to a search for the meaning of life. Alternatively she may be introduced to a person who is well versed in the Ancient Wisdom. This person will take on the role of a spiritual guide.

In this reading the Lagu Rune is reversed. This Rune represents the querant's present state of mind. She is naturally confused and muddled about the direction in which she wishes to direct her life energies. The Os Rune falling next to the reversed Lagu offers the way out of this confusion. This Rune is sacred to the hooded god Odin whose key qualities are wisdom, inspiration and communication. The Os Rune predicts that an older person will offer good counsel and sound advice to the querant. As a result of this her mental confusion will evaporate and she will be able to see the way forward more clearly. This clearing up of the psychic miasma surrounding the querant is further emphasized by the Cen Rune, representing illumination, and Sigil, which is the Rune of the Sun.

The final two Runes in the layout are Odal, the Ancestral Rune, and

Is, the Ice Rune. Odal is the Rune of completion. It signifies the end of the Quest on a spiritual level. In relation to this general reading it indicates that the right decision will be made and this will lead to the querant's happiness and peace of mind. The position of the Is Rune next to it does suggest that a few more obstacles will be placed in the querant's path before she reaches her final goal in life.

This general Rune reading can be summarized as follows. Its overall implication is that the querant is at an important crossroads in her life and in her self-development on a spiritual level. Major life decisions have to be taken but the Runes indicate that careful thought must be given to any decision which is made. There will be a successful outcome to a period of self doubt and confusion, and the querant will be helped by outsiders who are sympathetic to her goals. However the querant will need all her inner reservoirs of spiritual strength to face the challenges the Wyrd has in store for her. After a period of delay, and providing she keeps her head, the Runes foretell that everything will turn out to her advantage in the end.

In this general Rune reading it should be noted that, in most cases, the individual runic letters are not read separately. Wherever possible, each Rune is interpreted in relation to those in its immediate vicinity to give a clear predictive meaning. The interpretation of the Runes in this matter is a skill which obviously comes with practice. The apprentice Runecaster will soon learn how to interpret in this way and also how to relate individual Runes to the personal circumstances of the querant. Depending upon the querant, the Runecaster will know whether to offer a material interpretation of the Runes that have been laid out or to delve into their spiritual meaning. It is suggested that the would-be Runecaster does as many practice readings either for him- or herself or for relatives, in order to gain experience in runic interpretation before launching on a professional career.

If a specific answer to a question is required, then a shorter Rune reading can be done. In this second method five Rune stones or cards are selected from the bag or pack at random, after they have been thoroughly shuffled. The five Runes are laid out in a pattern which is known as as the Cross of Thor. It should not be thought that this cross design holds any Christian symbolism. The sign of the equal-armed cross predates the Christian religion by many thousands of years. It was a very important symbol in the pagan Old Religion and it is believed to be the original sigil from which the swastika or solar wheel developed. It is representative of the four elemental forces of earth, air, fire and water which meet in balanced harmony at the centre of the cross.

In order to provide a clearer indication of her future direction, the querant has asked a specific question relating to her employment prospects. We will use this question to illustrate a shorter Rune reading using the Cross of Thor layout. Using the cards on which the Runes are drawn, or Rune stones, we ask the querant to select four Runes from the pack or bag at random. As the querant selects the Runes she formulates in her mind the question she wishes to ask.

The four selected Runes are placed clockwise in the shape of an equal-armed cross on the casting cloth or table top. At the centre of the cross is placed a fifth Rune from the pack or bag. This is selected separately by the querant while she is concentrating on the question she wishes to have answered. We therefore have a pattern of Runes as illustrated below.

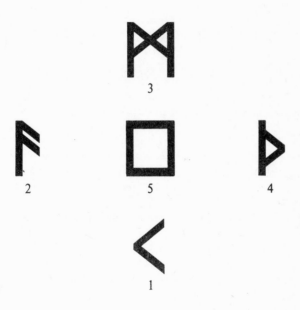

Moving Sunways (clockwise) around the Cross of Thor, the first Rune at the bottom represents the general influences surrounding the querant's enquiry. The second Rune, on the left-hand side of the cross in position 2, represents any obstacles facing the querant. The third Rune, at the top of the cross, is symbolic of the forces working in the querant's favour. On the right-hand side of the cross, in position 4, this Rune represents the short-term consequences of the reading on the querant's life. Finally the Rune in position 5, in the centre of the Cross of Thor, is the long-term influence of the reading on the life of the querant. It is the controlling influence on the layout.

In this second example, we will take each Rune individually and examine its meaning. A summary of the overall meaning of the reading as indicated by all five Runes will then be offered.

Rune 1 - Cen This is the Rune of spiritual illumination. On the mundane level it indicates that the querant will come into contact with people who are of a higher social standing than those she usually mixes with socially. These people will be instrumental in assisting her career prospects. As this Rune in this position on the Cross of Thor symbolizes the general influences surrounding the querant, they can be regarded as very beneficial to her progress.

Rune 2 - Os In the shorter reading this Rune represents the obstacles facing the querant. It indicates an older person who may offer advice on the choice of a career. This advice should be considered carefully for, with the Rune in this position, any suggestions made could well become an impediment to achieving the required goal.

Rune 3 - Man This indicates the forces working in the querant's favour. This Rune symbolizes either a person who is an official or a male member of the family. It indicates that help in choosing or gaining a new career will either come from male relatives of the querant or from a person working in local or national government or in a large business corporation. A certain amount of conflict with the outside world is indicated but the effects of this will be minimized because of the Rune's favourable position in the layout.

Rune 4 - Thorn The fourth Rune represents the short-term effect of the querant's question. An important decision will have to be made in the near future. Either a journey across water or a message from afar will have a bearing on this decision. The course of action taken will lead to the transformation of the querant's life.

Rune 5 - Wyrd This Rune is in the centre of the Cross and holds the key to the whole reading. It can be seen that the querant has selected the blank Rune of the Wyrd which is the most important symbol in the runic alphabet. The overall significance of this short reading is that the outcome of the question posed is in the hands of the querant. The Norns, the three goddesses in Norse mythology who are the personifications of the Wyrd, are working behind the scenes weaving their web of destiny. Events on the inner levels, which the querant may be only dimly aware of, are forming and will shortly become manifest on the physical plane of existence. Powerful forces are working in her favour and, providing she has the courage and strength to hang on, things will work out to her advantage in the end.

The reader will have noticed that some of the Runes in figures 1 and 2 overlap. As the two readings were completed within a short period of time, one would be very surprised if this were not the case.

As can be seen from the two examples above, a Rune reading offers guidance and advice but leaves the ultimate choice to the querant. Any form of divination which takes the power of free will and self determination away from the person who consults it, cannot be recommended. It is very easy for weak-willed persons to become 'prediction junkies', hooked on readings. One hears of business tycoons or showbiz personalities who will not move without first consulting their astrologer or Tarot reader. Any form of predictive counselling can only be a system of guidance and the ultimate decision rests with the querant. Predictive methods can help make that final decision easier, but they can never replace the divine gift of free will.

Our third example of a Rune reading is more complex than the others. It is known as the Runic Wheel. Again the pack or bag of Runes is shuffled and then thirteen Runes are selected at random either by the Runecaster or by the querant. These are laid out on the casting cloth in the shape of a wheel, beginning at the nine o'clock position and working clockwise around the circle until twelve Runes have been placed in position. The last Rune is placed in the centre of the wheel and represents the ruling influence of the spread. The Runes can then be interpreted either individually, in groups of three or in relation to their opposite number on the other side of the wheel. Each position is said by some Runecasters to have its own special meaning as follows.

First position Health matters
Second position Material possessions, finance and security
Third position Relationships between the querant and his or her
   family, relatives and intimate friends
Fourth position Home life and daily environment
Fifth position The creative arts, sport and games of chance
Sixth position The relationship between the querant and the outside
   world
Seventh position The relationship between querant and the opposite
   sex. If homosexual or bisexual, the querant's relationship with
   both sexes
Eighth position Gains through legacies or wills. May indicate the

nature of the querant's own death or the death of those close to him or her

Ninth position Travel, legal matters, religion and non-blood kin

Tenth position The querant's career and the best way he or she can establish him- or herself in the material world

Eleventh position The querant's social contacts and membership of clubs, societies, etc., and his or her hobbies

Twelfth position The secret life of the querant and his innermost desires and fantasies

As can be imagined, a very comprehensive Rune reading can be completed using this particular layout. How the Runes relate to the first position are given below as a guide to their interpretation within the Runic Wheel layout.

FEOH   *Upright:* Happiness. Good health
                    Reversed: Unhappiness. Minor health problems

UR   *Upright:* A person who is strong and healthy
                    Reversed: A weak person who suffers frequent illness

THORN   *Upright:* A warning of colds and chills
                    Reversed: Tendency for stress-related illnesses

OS   *Upright:* The querant should live to a good age
                    Reversed: The querant will suffer from age-related ailments in old age or will have to nurse an old person

RAD   *Upright:* The querant should take life more easily
                    Reversed: A trip to see a sick relative

CEN   *Upright:* The querant has an abundance of life energy
                    Reversed: A nervous breakdown or collapse of health

GYFU   *Upright:* The querant has the gift of good health
                    Reversed: Separation from loved ones due to illness

WYN   *Upright:* Joy and happiness
Reversed: Loss of affection from loved ones due to health problems

HAEGL   *Upright:* A serious illness
Reversed: Illness caused by accident

NYD   *Upright:* Illness related to stomach trouble
Reversed: Moderation is required if health is not to suffer

ISR   *Upright:* Emotional stagnation. Impotence. Frigidity
Reversed: Sterility

EOH   *Upright:* Protection from illness
Reversed: Breakdown of body's natural defences

SIGIL   *Upright:* Good health and vitality. Sexual vigour
Reversed: A warning to take life as it comes

TYR   *Upright:* Venereal disease
Reversed: Sexual frustration

BEORC   *Upright:* A birth in the family
Reversed: Miscarriage. Abortion. Difficult birth

PEORTH   *Upright:* Suggests querant should have medical consultation or check up
Reversed: A warning to seek urgent medical advice

EOLH   *Upright:* Prevention is better than cure
Reversed: Ditto

EH ᛗ *Upright:* Health problems connected with moving house or changing career
Reversed: Ditto

MAN ᛉ *Upright:* Illness among male relatives
Reversed: Illness which will isolate querant from the outside world

LAGU ᛚ *Upright:* A trip to see a relative across water
Reversed: Mental illness

ING ᛜ *Upright:* End of a cycle. Recovery from illness
Reversed: Ditto

DAEG *Upright:* Health improvements after a period of prolonged illness
Reversed: Change of material circumstances for worst caused by long-standing health problems

ODAL ᛟ *Upright:* News of old people who are sick
Reversed: Hereditary illness

The Runic Wheel layout is ideal if a comprehensive reading is required to cover a wide range of problems or factors affecting the querant.

We mentioned earlier in this chapter the ethical aspect of Runecasting. This is a subject we would like to return to as it is a very important aspect of predictive Runecraft. The Runecaster is in a position of trust in relation to the person who is consulting him or her. The relationship between the Runecaster and the querant is confidential and is akin to that between a doctor and his patient. As stated before, those people who consult fortune tellers do so because they are usually seeking help with emotional, financial or health problems. To these people the future may seem like a black void, and it is the task of the competent Runecaster to shine a light forward into the murky darkness so that the shadow of future events can be discerned.

In order to help such people, the Runecaster must have some knowledge of human nature and basic psychology. He or she must be a good listener and be able to communicate easily with people of all social classes. The querant must feel at ease during the reading and be reassured that any confidential information he or she may reveal about his or her private life will remain secret once the consultation is ended. When the querant confides his innermost desires and fears to the Runecaster, there must be the understanding that anything revealed will not be passed on to a third party.

The emotional problems about which the querant consults the Runecaster will often concern the imminent breakup of a marriage or a sexual relationship or a marital tangle. If the querant is single, divorced or separated, he may be infatuated with someone who does not return his affection. In such circumstances it is essential for the Runecaster to display tact and refrain from any attempt to preach morality. Obviously any observations made about the problem will be based on the Runes selected by the querant. However, a commonsensical, down-to-earth approach to the problem by the Runecaster will do much to calm any potentially dangerous emotional disturbance. Dealing with emotional problems is one facet of Runecraft in which the psychic faculty of the Runecaster has its uses.

It is not a prerequisite of Runecasting to be psychically aware but it helps. Some gifted people are naturally sensitive to psychic perceptions. It requires very little effort by such people to tune in to the vibrations of their clients. The Rune symbols act as a focus for the Runecaster's own psychic powers. It should be remembered that the Rune meanings given in this book are not dogma. Meditation on the Runes may reveal other meanings which are just as valid and can be adopted by the skilled Runecaster in his or her predictive analysis.

We are all, to a lesser or greater extent, psychic. When you encounter a dyed-in-the-wool materialist it is very difficult to accept that as a fact. However, if you probe deep enough you will find that even the most rational, materially orientated person has experienced at least one strange happening in his life which even he cannot logically explain. In addition, we all share archetypal atavistic emotions such as a fear of spiders, which is a throwback to a period in our evolution (using that word in its widest sense) when we were more aware. The degeneration of the psychic sense can be directly linked to our material progress, which has been at the expense of our spirituality. Gradually over the centuries we have been building a totally artificial environment in which we live for the greater part of our lives. We have effectively closed ourselves off from the natural, organic environment in which our ancestors lived.

The Northern European people who used the Rune system were in daily contact with the elemental forces of nature in a way that few people today ever experience. The nearest we come to their level of natural awareness may be on a rambling or camping holiday, but even that is for a short period of time. Few campers nowadays are far from the sophisticated comforts of our materialistic society. This contact with nature is essential if psychic powers are to be developed. Excellent psychics can live in busy city centres, but fresh air, open spaces and contact with feral things are essential requirements for any would-be Runecaster seeking awareness of the hidden side of life. We should remember that the ancient shamans experienced their secret initiation rites into the mysteries after a period of isolation in contact with the natural world of the elements.

It has been suggested that the Runes (or any other form of predictive tool) cannot produce an accurate reading by proxy. Many people do not have local access to readers and have to send away for postal readings. In such cases it is the psychic perception of the Runecaster which provides the link between the reader and the querant. Vibrations from a letter can be tuned in to by the Runecaster (or Tarot reader, etc.) and a rapport established with the absent client. Although the querant cannot select the Runes, the caster can tune in to them and make the selection on the querant's behalf.

One final word on ethics before we proceed to the more spiritual aspects of the Rune system and Northern European religion. Sometimes the Runecaster will perceive indications of death in a reading. This may be the death of the querant or somebody close to him. The dilemma arises as to whether the Runecaster should advise his client of the imminent event. As any psychiatrist will tell you, the mind is a very powerful weapon for good or bad. By revealing the knowledge he has to the querant the Runecaster may even precipitate the event. Autosuggestion is a potent force, especially if the querant is already depressed or emotionally insecure.

Even in our so-called permissive society (which in actuality is probably one of the most sexually repressed in history) death is the final taboo. Few people, unless they have a very strong religious conviction, ever come to terms with the eventual reality of their own death. It is something which happens every day but is seldom discussed in polite society. A person who tries to introduce the subject of coping with death, either one's own or others', into everyday conversation is likely to be treated like a social leper. Doctors faced with telling the terminally ill of their fate may not do so because of the strain this imposes on both the person concerned and those around him. For these reasons, until our society adopts a more enlightened approach to death, the Runecaster would be advised to take a similiar line.

Part Three

THE SPIRIT OF THE RUNES

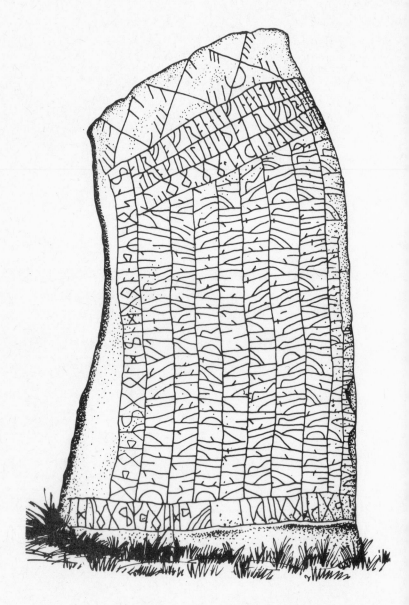

Swedish standing stone inscribed with runic symbols

7

A comprehensive study of the Runes, whether for divination or for spiritual use, cannot be made without placing the Rune system in the context of the religious beliefs of the society in which it flourished. Although frequently used for secular purposes, the runic alphabet was a key to unlocking esoteric symbolism. An understanding how these symbols work can only be achieved by examining the spiritual beliefs and religious practices of the people who used them.

In any study of the religious concepts of the pagan pre-Christian tribes of Northern Europe it is difficult to establish exactly when the Runes became the mystical alphabet that we know today. The religious ideas that we find encapsulated in the symbols of the Rune system had emerged in European culture in the early prehistoric period. They had naturally been refined and altered over the centuries, but their spiritual essence remained undiluted. Our first real knowledge of Scandinavian pagan beliefs emerged in the late nineteenth and early twentieth centuries when remains of Bronze Age people and their culture were unearthed from burial sites in Denmark. From archaeological data relating to the early Bronze Age we know that the major deity in the contemporary religious pantheon was a male god representing the sun. Both in rock carvings and burial artifacts, the theme of a sacred horse drawing the sun in a wagon across the sky predominates. This image is of Indo-European origin and also features in Hindu and Greek mythology. Another major symbol of sun worship dating from this period is the equal-armed cross and the eight-spoked sun wheel. Both of these symbols later developed into the swastika.

In the later Bronze Age we find more evidence of the cult of the Great Mother Goddess. Her consort was the Horned God who is depicted with an erect penis. He may be the forerunner of Frey or even of Odin, who is sometimes shown with horns. The worship of the Horned God was widespread in prehistoric, Bronze and Iron Age Europe. Identical effigies of the Horned One are to be found as far apart as on the Gundestrup cauldron excavated in Sweden, on a pagan altar under the crypt of Notre Dame cathedral in Paris, and at

Mohenjodaro in the Indus valley. In each case the Horned God is depicted with stag antlers and sits crosslegged surrounded by animals. Some experts have linked the European Horned God with Shiva, the ithyphallic Hindu god who was also known as the Lord of Animals.

Many of the religious rites of the Bronze Age Scandinavians were concerned with fertility and agriculture. Rock carvings depict magical rites in which a man with an erect penis is ploughing a field. Such rites were evidently performed in the spring to ensure a good harvest later in the season. These fertility practices survived in folklore in the belief that a naked woman pulling a plough around a field would ensure a fruitful harvest. In Germany only a few hundred years ago the first field of each farm to be ploughed in the new season was dug with a plough drawn by unmarried girls. In an even more sublimated version, the Bronze Age fertility rites survive in the Christian festival of Plough Sunday, when the priest blesses the ploughs.

Worship of the Great Goddess was as widespread in pagan Scandinavia as the celebration of rites to the masculine solar principle. Archaeologists have found numerous female figurines representing either the goddess or the priestesses of her cult. These figurines depict long-haired naked women, or women wearing short, corded skirts, with exposed breasts. Some wear large round earrings and necklaces which seem to have a ritual significance. Others seem to be holding or displaying their breasts in what may be a symbolic gesture of fecundity. The goddess or priestess figure is often seen in close proximity to a snake or to a representation of the Horned God or his human priest. In the late Bronze Age it is evident that the central religious beliefs of Northern Europe involved the worship of the Great Goddess who personified the earth and the Horned God who symbolized the sun.

When we examine the religious beliefs and the mythological pantheon of gods and goddesses worshipped in Northern Europe in the period when the Runes were in use – a period from the first century CE to the eleventh century CE – we find that the symbols and concepts of prehistoric and Bronze Age religion are easily recognizable, albeit in a more sophisticated form. Any form of religious belief is an attempt by the human mind to create order from a chaotic universe. It is common for modern religious scholars when writing about the history of spirituality to regard all early pagan beliefs as a primitive or barbaric phase in human consciousness. Even those students of comparative religion who concede that the pagan world view is a valid philosophy reserve their praise for the classical spirituality of Greece.

In fact, the Celtic, Norse and Saxon forms of religion offer a rich tapestry of belief which is far from barbaric or primitive, even though it may seem so to our modern intellectuals.

Our knowledge of the central tenets of Northern European paganism owes a tremendous debt to the Icelandic scholar Snorri Sturluson. In his classic work, which was published under the title of *The Gølda* in 1220, he outlined the central tenets of Northern European pagan religion. Snorri wrote his book at a time when the last surviving practices of the Old Faith were being threatened by the new religion of Christianity. His aim was that of a modern folklorist, to capture the old myths before they faded from memory. Because he was writing in a society which had recently embraced the new faith he was reluctant to confer the status of divinity on the personalities who starred in the myths he recorded. In Snorri's opinion, the Norse gods and goddesses were of human origin. The storm god Thor was the grandson of King Priam of Troy. One of Thor's sons was Odin who, with his sister/wife Freya, travelled north from Greece to Denmark, Sweden and Norway. In each country he left a son as ruler. This parallels the theory discussed earlier that Odin or Woden was a shaman who invented the runic alphabet and was deified after his ritual death.

The widespread view propagated by the medieval Church was that the old pagan gods and goddesses were demons in disguise. Snorri wisely rejected this notion, but he was not brave enough to tell his readership that the old gods were legitimate representations of divinity. He therefore presented the gods as superhuman heroes who were deified in the folk memory of the cultures which inherited the tales concerning them. In this way Snorri escaped any charge by the Church that he was supporting devil worship by writing about the pagan myths and legends. As far as he was concerned, the gods led lives very similar to human beings but on a grander scale. This approach to the Norse myths was naturally regarded with a considerable amount of cynicism by scholars and clerics who did not understand the allegorical nature of pagan mythology.

In his detailed account Snorri describes how an early Swedish king welcomes Odin on his arrival in the country. The king later travels to the halls of the Aesir (the name for Odin's family) to discover the truth about the stranger. In the halls he meets a triad of mysterious beings who relate the creation myths and names of the gods and goddesses of the Nordic pantheon.

When the Indo-Europeans (the Celts and the ancestors of the Vikings) colonized Western and Northern Europe they absorbed many of the religious beliefs and practices of the aboriginal tribes whom they conquered. The elements of pre-Celtic and pre-Viking spirituality which we describe earlier were manifest again in Norse and Germanic religious practices. While it is true that the Norse gods and goddesses became humanized, they can still be identified with the deities worshipped in prehistoric and early Bronze Age times. The Old Religion adapted to cultural circumstances but its essential elements remained constant over a period of many thousands of years. It is for this reason that when the Romans encountered the Celts and the Germani they recognized the tribal gods as equivalents to their own classical pantheon of divine beings. In fact, the Roman persecution of the Celtic Druids was not, as some historians would have us believe, on the grounds of their religious practices but because they were organizing political resistance to the occupying troops.

We begin our examination of the Norse myths with the story of creation as related in the old legends. From primordial chaos arose two regions. One, situated in the south, was filled with bright light and was ruled by the elemental power of cosmic fire. The second region was composed of darkness and was ruled by the elemental power of cosmic ice. In the vast emptiness of space between the two zones where the heat and the cold met, a gigantic archetypal being known as Ymir appeared in the melting ice. From under his left arm grew the first man and woman, while from his feet sprang the elven race of frost giants. Ymir was nourished by the sacred cow Auohumla, who licked an ice block and released another human called Buri. Cows were sacred to the Indo-Europeans as they are today to the Hindus. Cows are also related to the Feoh Rune which has the symbolic meaning of 'cattle'.

Buri had a son called Bor and he in turn had three sons known as Vili, Ve and Odin. These three beings killed Ymir and from his dead body they created Midgard or Middle Earth, which is the world of humankind. From his flesh they made the earth, from his blood the sea and from his bones the mountains. The skull of Ymir was used to form the dome of the sky with a dwarf at each corner to support it. From Ymir's eyebrows the three sons of Bor made a wall to protect Midgard from attack by the frost giants. They also created the dwarves who live under the earth. These goblin creatures made all the weapons and treasures used by the gods from solid gold which they mined from under the hills of Middle Earth. Ymir's name, incidentally, has been said to derive from the Sanscrit word *yama*, which means 'hermaphrodite'. The concept of the creator god as an adrogynous or dual-sexed being is common to the myths of many diverse pagan belief systems apart from the Norse one.

At first glance this creation myth seems to be a simplistic fairy tale. To a certain extent all such myths must be evaluated on that superficial level, even the Judeo-Christian creation recounted in Genesis. However, these apparently fanciful stories have to be interpreted on a symbolic level as allegorical fables explaining the origin of the universe. In the Norse creation myth we have two cosmic forces, fire and ice, ruling the universe prior to the arrival of humanity. Mythologically, these forces are sometimes personified by twin gods known as the Alcis who were worshipped by the Germanic tribes. Tacitus describes their worship as being carried out in forest sanctuaries by their priesthood who dressed in women's clothing.

The two opposing cosmic forces of fire and ice are comparable to the Yin and Yang principles found in ancient Chinese Taoism. They represent the polarity of the life force which is manifest in the material universe as light and darkness, masculine and feminine, good and evil, etc. These forces are in an eternal state of conflict, but their interaction brings the physical plane into existence and sustains it as a separate reality. These two opposing forces can be transcended, for there is only one power which is responsible for the creation. This is the life force, which first divides into two – the Yin–Yang or Fire–Ice combination – and then into the myriad of different forms which compose the physical universe. In the pagan myths these different aspects of the life force manifesting through the medium of the natural world are personified as gods and goddesses. This is the esoteric truth behind the old maxim: 'All the Gods are one God'.

From the viewpoint of a pagan animist, all life forms and the material world are permeated by the life force. Our ancestors believed that all animate and inanimate objects in the physical world were possessed of a divine soul. This is why in the oldest pagan myths we find such a multiplicity of different gods and goddesses representing trees, hills, rivers and animals. With the coming of Christianity these minor gods were at first transformed into nature spirits or faeries and then condemned as devils.

When the Christian missionaries preached their sermons against the Norse gods they compared Ymir and the frost giants to the legendary giants of biblical lore. In *Beowulf* mention is made of a race of northern giants and dark elves who were born of Cain and battled with God. They were eventually drowned for their sins. In the Bible we are told that the mysterious Sons of God came down to earth and mated with the daughters of humankind. The resulting offspring were giants who were skilled in sorcery. Their wickedness eventually forced God to destroy humanity in a great deluge, saving only Noah, his family and a zoo to repopulate the world. The Sons of God are also known as the Watchers or Fallen Angels who taught humankind the arts of civilization.

The major cosmological symbol of Norse and Germanic mythology is the sacred World Tree known as Yggdrasil. Trees have always been important in the pagan shamanistic religion. According to ancient shamanistic belief, the sacred World Tree passes through the nine worlds or heavens. In the Norse and Germanic versions of the pagan Old Religion the sacred World Tree is usually an ash. It is a symbol of life, time and destiny, and its branches embrace the whole universe. It is a cosmic symbol representing the unity of all life.

The three roots of the tree are formed in the spiritual, terrestrial and infernal realms of existence. The spiritual root has its source in Asgard, the home of the Aesir deities. This root is watered by a sacred spring guarded by the Norns, the goddesses of the Wyrd. The terrestrial root has its source in Midgard or Middle Earth, which is the domain of humankind. It is watered by the well of Mimir which traditionally grants anyone who drinks from it the gift of divine wisdom. When Odin came to drink from the well Mimir demanded that the hooded god sacrifice one of his eyes before he would allow him to drink. When Mimir was killed by the Vanir gods, Odin travelled to the well to seek oracular advice from Mimir's severed head. The infernal root has its source in Niflheim which is the abode of the dead and has a sacred spring guarded by a dragon.

The three branches of the World Tree support Middle Earth, in the centre of which rises a sacred mountain where the gods live. This is very similiar to Mount Olympus in Greek mythology, which is the legendary home of the classical gods and goddesses. In the sea surrounding Middle Earth is a huge serpent with its tail in its mouth. This is a very ancient symbol of eternity found in many Eastern religions. The home of the gods on the sacred peak is joined to the three roots by the Rainbow Bridge so that the gods can travel up and down the tree whenever they please.

In the uppermost branches of the tree various sacred animals live. On the very top branch perches an eagle, which represents higher wisdom. Between his eyes sits a hawk whose penetrating eyes can see into every corner of the universe. Odin's goat Heidrim feeds on the evergreen leaves of the tree and four stags also graze in the upper branches, dripping honey from their antlers. A squirrel called Ratatosk scampers up and down the branches of the tree carrying messages from the eagle to the dragon of Niflheim. Serpents are sacred to the Great Mother Goddess, while the eagle represents the masculine cosmic principle. The squirrel messenger symbolizes the shaman who travels between the nine worlds and communicates with the spirit realms.

Of the worlds symbolically represented on the World Tree the most important is probably Asgard, inhabited by the Aesir gods. In this world exist many huge halls lavishly decorated in gold and silver. Odin dwells within a hall whose walls are encrusted with precious stones and which has a silver-plated roof. Another hall within Asgard is Valhalla, where the souls of the warriors who have died in battle with a sword in their hands are carried by Odin's handmaidens, the Valkyries. There the fallen heroes feast on a never ending supply of the finest meat and drink mead from horns which never run dry.

After Odin the principal god of the Aesir is the storm god Thor. According to Adam of Bremen, Thor 'ruled the sky, governed thunder, wind and storms, fair weather and the fruits of the earth'. Thor is the archetypal sky god of the Indo-European religious tradition. He is the champion of Aesir and defender of Asgard from its enemies. He appears as a giant, red-bearded figure, riding across the sky in a chariot drawn by goats and surrounded by thunder clouds. He wears an iron girdle which increases his physical strength a hundredfold, iron gloves, and carries a magical stone hammer called Mjollnir which when thrown at enemies returns to his hand like a boomerang. The Romans identified Thor with Zeus, Jupiter and Hercules.

Thor is constantly involved in heroic adventures in his role as defender of Asgard. Some of these escapades give the impression that he is slightly dim-witted, but this is a device to illustrate his supernatural strength. For instance, when Thor encounters the king of the giants the latter challenges him to a series of tests. First, Thor struggles in vain to drain a moderately sized drinking horn. He takes three enormous mouthfuls, but it seems just as full as when he began. Second, the king tells Thor to pick up his cat, which the god is unable to do. Lastly, the giant challenges Thor to a wrestling match with an old woman but the thunder god loses.

When all the challenges are completed the king reveals to Thor that he has been suffering from a spell of enchantment. In the first contest the drinking horn had an open end and had been placed in the sea. Thor had in fact lowered the ocean by a few inches with his mighty draughts. In the second the cat Thor could not lift was the World

Serpent which lies coiled around Middle Earth. In the last the ancient crone Thor had lost the wrestling match to was old age whom nobody can beat.

Although Thor can be dismissed as a comic figure the emphasis is always on his strength and courage. He represents the destructive force of the elements harnessed for positive ends. His hammer symbolizes this force; the double-headed axe or hammer has always been a sacred weapon from its earliest depictions in prehistoric art. As we have seen, the Romans regarded Thor as a Nordic version of Hercules or Herakles. In a way very similiar to that of the Norse thunder god, Hercules battles with monsters representing the forces of evil and carries a huge club which resembles Thor's magical hammer. The hill figure of the giant outlined in chalk above the Dorset village of Cerne Abbas has been identified as Hercules. He has a huge erect phallus and is waving a club. Other experts have claimed that the giant represents Dagda, who was the father sky god of the Celts. Both Hercules and Dagda share similar attributes with Thor.

The third important god among the Aesir is Baldur, son of Odin and Frigga, the goddess of love. This deity is sometimes called Baldur the Beautiful and his aura is said to glow with a holy light. He is obviously a solar deity, the Norse equivalent of the shining god Lugh in Celtic mythology and Helios–Apollo in the Graeco-Roman pagan religion. According to the Nordic myths, the beautiful young god was troubled by nightmares predicting his premature death. His mother Frigga asked every animate and inaminate thing in Middle Earth to promise never to harm Baldur. She hoped by this promise to prevent any harm coming to the god. Water, fire, earth, stones, trees, animals, fish and birds all agreed to Frigga's request because of their great love and respect for the goddess. It has been suggested that this story reveals Frigga as the personification of Mother Earth. Certainly she was the goddess of venereal love, for her name survives today in the slang word for female masturbation.

Unfortunately, among the gods of the Aesir Baldur had a rival who resented his youth and beauty. This rival was Loki, the god of fire, who is the nearest thing to a principle of evil in the Norse myths. He was later identified with the Devil by the medieval Church but it would be incorrect to see him as a Satanic or demonic character. His daughter Hel was banished by Odin to Niflheim which was a place of shadows and mists. There she presided over the realm of the dead.

Motivated by envy, Loki disguised himself as an old woman and gained the confidence of Frigga. He discovered that the goddess of love had managed to obtain an oath from all things in Middle Earth promising not to hurt her son, except for the humble mistletoe because it looked too young to do any harm. In order to prove that Baldur could not be injured or killed, the gods played a game. Each took turns to throw spears, stones and other objects at the young god. Loki quickly found some mistletoe and from the twig made a set of darts. He then persuaded the blind god Holdur to throw these deadly missiles at the young god. Baldur immediately fell to the ground dead. All the gods lamented the death of Baldur, and the earth and all its creatures wept for him. Baldur was eventually reborn, and therefore his myth parallels those of Middle Eastern saviour gods such as Attis, Adonis and Christ.

However, Baldur was not reborn immediately after his death like other resurrection gods. His rebirth was as a result of the cataclysmic event in Northern European mythology known as Ragnarok. In German this is translated as *Gotterdammerung* or the Twilight of the Gods. Ragnarok will be preceded by a great winter which will last for three years, followed by earthquakes, famine and the release of the frost giants to plague Middle Earth. In this period hatred will exist among all races, the bonds of kinship will become meaningless, and murder and incest will be widespread. During the great winter the Fenris Wolf will become loosed from its shackles and devour the sun. The sacred World Tree will shake from its branches to its roots, mountains will tumble into the sea and the whole of Middle Earth will tremble.

In the final days Odin will ride out of Asgard with his Valkyries and the mighty gods of the Aesir to do battle with the Fenris Wolf and the frost giants. During this final ultimate battle all the gods and the giants are destroyed. 'The Sun becomes dark. The Earth sinks into the sea. The shining stars slip out of the sky. Vapour and fire rage fiercely together until the leaping flames lick heaven.' All is not lost though, for this orgy of cosmic destruction is for a reason: Ragnarok is the process by which a new order is created in the universe. The earth rises green and shining from the sea, the sun appears in the sky again, Baldur is reborn and rules over a new Asgard cleansed of its impurities. Two mortals who have been hiding in the branches of Yggdrasil creep out to repopulate Middle Earth. New hills rise from the ebbing flood water and trees and flowers bloom again. Nature is renewed and the cycle of death and rebirth begins anew.

In addition to Odin, Thor, Tyr the war god, Frigga and Baldur, there are several other lesser-known gods of the Aesir. One of the most mysterious is Mimir, the guardian of the sacred well of wisdom.

Attempts have been made to prove that Mimir's name comes from the Latin *memor* which gives us our English word 'memory'. Other etymologists have traced Mimir to the Anglo-Saxon *meotud,* meaning 'fate', which would link the god with the Norns. The sacred well of Mimir has symbolic similarities to the Cauldron of Rebirth and Inspiration in Celtic mythology. The fact that Mimir's head is utilized as an oracle reminds us how the head of Bran the Blessed was carried by his warriors from Ireland to burial at the White Mount in London and talked all the way. The cult of the sacred head was an important aspect of Celtic religious belief.

Mimir has a companion who is equally as mysterious as the guardian of the sacred well of wisdom. He is called Hoenir and is said to have been present at the creation when humanity was given the gift of intelligence. He is one of the few gods to survive Ragnarok and rule in the new order. He is generally said to be silent, which was an attribute widely prized by the North Europeans as a sign of great wisdom.

Another odd figure in the Norse myths is Heimdall, the guardian of the Rainbow Bridge linking Asgard with Middle Earth and the Underworld on the World Tree. Heimdall requires no sleep, can see in the dark and has supernormal hearing. He carries a special horn which he blows as a warning of danger. Although he is said to belong to the Aesir, this god also has connections with the rival divine dynasty of the Vanir. It is doubtful if he is related to them, but as he shares their hidden knowledge and is a watcher between heaven and the Underworld, he is associated with the Vanir gods. In some legends Heimdall is even called 'the father of the human race', suggesting that at some period he was a far more important divine being.

The differences between the Aesir and the Vanir are quite considerable. The Aesir are a race or dynasty of warlike sky gods whose origins can be found in Indo-European religious tradition. Their elemental symbols are fire and wind. On the other side, the Vanir are fertility and nature deities who were worshipped by the aboriginal inhabitants of Northern Europe conquered by the Aryans. Their elemental symbols are earth and water.

At some historical period the two pantheons merged. In mythological terms the Vanir and the Aesir waged war on each other and then made an uneasy truce. The goddess Skadi, wife of the Vanir sea god Njord, bore children to Odin to unite the bond between the two divine races. In Norse mythology the Vanir are associated with the powers of darkness, fertility, the elemental forces of nature and the cult of the dead. They are amoral gods who are not interested in the higher spiritual aspirations of their human worshippers but provide fertility in the fields and the home. In addition, the Vanir provide mortals with the power to communicate with the spirit world, predict the future and perform magic.

8

The gods and goddesses of the Vanir are primarily deities of fertility and nature. The chief deities of the Vanir are a god and goddess called Frey and Freya, whose names mean respectively 'Lord' and 'Lady'. Frey is a male fertility god and his statues excavated by archaeologists depict a gnomish figure, sitting crosslegged, wearing a pointed cap and with a large erect penis. He is the god of plenty and the harvest, whose major festival was held at the end of August. Frey's worship involved ritual sex acts, religious prostitution, dancing, sacred marriages and men dressed as women. Weapons were not allowed in Frey's temples, no blood could be shed within their precincts and no outlaw could enter his sanctuary.

In early pagan times in Sweden the king was regarded as the human representative of Frey and was symbolically married to a priestess of the Great Mother Goddess. At an appointed time it is surmised that these priest kings suffered a ritual death in order to promote the fertility of the land. There are several historical instances of kings meeting with violent deaths which cannot be rationally explained. Dr Margaret Murray has suggested that the ritual killing of kings as representatives of a fertility god survived into the Middle Ages. Her theory although interesting remains unproven for obvious reasons.

The sacred animals of Frey are the boar and the horse. Helmets and masks in the shape of a boar's face have been found dating from the Viking Age and may have been used for ceremonial purposes. The boar is regarded in popular country belief as a very virile animal and is therefore the perfect symbol for a fertility god. A white boar was the personal heraldic symbol of the hunchbacked King Richard III who was the last of the Plantagenet dynasty. According to Dr Margaret Murray again, the Plantagenets are supposed to have been secret followers of the pagan Old Religion. They were of Norman French stock and the Normans were originally Norse pirates who were granted land in France.

The other animal sacred to Frey is the horse. We have seen in our examination of the Eh Rune that horses were sacred to the Indo-

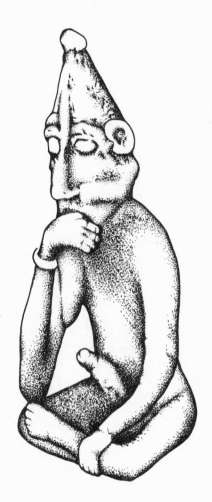

FREY
Phallic god of fertility

Europeans and was greatly venerated in pagan Scandinavia and Germany. The harvest festival of Frey often featured horse racing and what are described as 'horse fights'. A relic of the sexual rites associated with Frey is related in one of the tales of the Christian saint Olaf. He visited a farm in a remote part of Norway and was horrified to find the farmer's wife worshipped the penis of a stallion which she kept preserved with herbs and wrapped in a fine linen cloth. Every night the family passed this sacred object from hand to hand and recited pagan incantations. The shocked saint confiscated the phallus and fed it to the family dog! He then proceeded to teach the heathen family the error of their pagan ways and converted them to the new faith.

The other principal festival associated with Frey was the ritual mating of a priest and priestess in the springtime. During this rite the couple were regarded as the human personifications of the Lord and Lady. This sexual rite survives today in a very watered-down version as the traditional English custom of crowing a King and Queen of the May at Mayday celebrations.

Frey's sister and wife is Freya, the goddess of fertility, sexuality and childbirth. Although such incestuous arrangements are difficult for us to understand with our modern taboo on sexual relationships between blood relatives, there are many instances of brother and sister marriages in pagan mythology. Only rarely did this sexual licence extend to the worshippers of the gods in question. One notable exception was in ancient Egypt where brothers and sisters (and sometimes mothers and sons) married to preserve the 'pure blood' of the Pharaohs. Unfortunately, due to the genetic disorders which can arise in babies born of such relationships, the Pharaohs achieved the opposite effect and doomed their royal dynasty to extinction.

Freya is the goddess who rules fertility and has a vociferous sexual appetite. She is said to have obtained a magical necklace by sleeping with the four dwarves who forged it in one night. Necklaces were very important religious objects in the pagan Old Religion, as we have already seen. Although Freya is associated with the fertility rites and sexual fun-and-games of her brother's worship, she is a slightly more complex deity than this at first suggests. She is in fact an aspect of the Triple Goddess whose worship was so widespread among the Celtic peoples. This Triple Goddess has three aspects, characterized as the Maiden or Enchantress, the Great Mother and the Old Crone. In pagan lore the Maiden is associated with divination, magical rites, clairvoyance and enchantment; the Great Mother is linked with fertility, sexuality and childbirth; and finally, the Old Crone is connected with death, the Otherworld and rebirth.

Because of the merging of the two divine families of the Aesir and the Vanir it is difficult to separate the attributes of the different gods and goddesses. Certainly the Aesir borrowed many of the powers credited to the Vanir. It has been suggested that the Triple Goddess was originally represented by Freya, Frigga and Skadi the goddess of the hunt. Both Freya and Frigga were said to rule over childbirth, sexual love and fertility, so it is possible that they were originally one goddess. Skadi was married to both Njord, the Vanir god of the sea, and also to Odin, the Aesir Allfather, suggesting a union between the two divine families.

The mother of both Frey and Freya is Nerthus, who is the Earth Mother of Northern European myth. Tacitus in his book *Germania* describes her worship among the tribes inhabiting northern Germany and Scandinavia. According to the Roman historian, the sacred grove of Nerthus was on an island in the sea or on a lake. Her effigy sat in a sacred wagon covered by a veil. Only one priest was allowed to touch the wagon and walk beside it when it was carried to land for her festival. During this ritual there was no war and every weapon was put away. This state of peace lasted as long as the effigy of the goddess was away from its sacred grove.

Brian Branston in his book *The Lost Gods of England* suggests that the grotesque carvings known as sheela-na-gigs found in old Norman churches may be representations of Freya or Nerthus. The sheela-na-gigs are gargoyles in female shape with exaggerated sexual organs. Often they crouch with their legs open displaying their cunni to public view. The purpose of the sheela-na-gigs in churches is unknown but their blatant sexual poses would seem to indicate that they are of pagan rather than Christian origin.

Although the Normans were nominally Christian and built many churches in England after 1066, many of these clerical buildings are crammed with pagan symbols. As well as the sheela-na-gigs, many Norman churches display carvings of the Green Man. He is a medieval version of the old pagan gods of the wood worshipped by the Romans as Faunus, by the Greeks as Pan and by the Celts as Cernunnos. Shortly before the Norman Conquest the Saxon Church had been forced to issue edicts condemning the worship of trees, stones, the stars, the sun and the moon, and forbidding the practice of wiccaecraft or witchcraft. This suggests that the pagan Old Religion was still actively practised in the countryside. When William the Conqueror was hunting down the Saxon rebel Hereward the Wake in the fens of

East Anglia, he employed a witch to chant curses from a wooden tower. Unfortunately for the witch, the Saxon rebels crept up to the base of the tower and set it alight, burning her to death. William obviously used this device because he thought the Saxon rebels had a superstitious fear of witchcraft and enchantment.

Although Freya is the goddess of fertility and childbirth, paradoxically she is also the goddess of the dead and the spirit world. She is the leader of the Disir, a group of mysterious female deities related to Odin's host of Valkyries who ride with the Wild Hunt. The Disir were placated with sacrifices by the peasantry at their festival, celebrated in February. They have the ability to foretell the death of members of the family and seem to be very similar to the Irish banshees of Celtic lore.

Snorri writes that Freya rides to battle and gathers up one half of the corpses of the slain, while Odin takes the other half. This collecting the souls of dead warriors is usually associated with the Valkyries/Disir, so we can safely assume that Freya has ultimate control over these female spirits of death. In one of the old Scandinavian sagas a would-be suicide is quoted as saying: 'I shall take no food until I sup with Freya', which again suggests she is the goddess of the dead. Traditionally, both Frey and Freya are said to have dominion over the elemental realm of elves, goblins and faeries.

In her alternative aspect as the Maiden goddess, Freya is the weaver of enchantments, the mistress of dark magic and the caster of spells. It is even said that Freya taught these arts to Odin and the other gods of the Aesir. This seems to confirm the fact that the worship of the Vanir deities was far older and had its roots in the magico-religious rituals and practices of prehistoric shamanism.

Freya also shares with Odin the magical power of shape changing. This technique is accomplished by means of a cloak of falcon feathers. Using this garment, Freya can change into a bird and fly between Middle Earth and the Otherworld. In one story, Loki, the god of fire, borrows Freya's magic cloak to fly to the land of the frost giants.

In his account of the Norse gods and goddesses Snorri says that Freya was an expert at a special form of magical working known as *seior*. In a previous chapter we read of the Rune Mistresses from contemporary accounts. They were evidently practitioners of this magical art and placed themselves in a trance by singing special sacred songs. While in this mediumistic state they answered questions about the future. The answers given were believed to originate from the goddess Freya herself. These priestesses of the cult of Freya were known as *volvas*, which is a term meaning 'one who can foresee the future'.

One incident involving the practice of *seior* involved a young Christian woman who was asked at a gathering to recite the sacred songs. She admitted that she had been taught these as a child but was reluctant to sing them since her conversion. Having been persuaded that it was not a sin, she duly complied with the request. Afterwards she was congratulated on her magical expertise because her singing had been so talented that crowds of spirits had entered the room from the Otherworld.

After the *volvas* had awoken from their trance state they were given a good meal and small gifts by the people who had been lucky enough to have received messages or advice. These priestesses were held in high esteem by the community and some were even regarded as Freya incarnate and worshipped as goddesses. There were darker aspects to the activities of these priestesses, for magic is a neutral force in itself and can be used for both positive and negative ends. When the Saxon bishops sought to eradicate paganism from the English countryside they denounced the use of magical practices which allegedly caused harm to others.

With Freya we have a classic example of the Triple Goddess who is more usually associated with the Celtic forms of the pagan Old Religion. She is an Earth Mother figure presiding over erotic rites of fertility to revive nature after its winter hibernation. She is the enchantress weaving magical spells and teaching the Ancient Wisdom to the mighty ones of the Aesir. She is the Old Crone who is the ruler of death, guardian of the Underworld and prophetess of the future. Freya is the eternal personification of the cosmic feminine principle of the life force worshipped by our pagan ancestors for thousands of years under many names and with many faces.

In addition to Frey and Freya, there are several other gods who play an important role in the Vanir dynasty. One of these is their father Njord who is the god of the sea. He was the patron of fishermen because he could control the waves and the wind. In the Viking Age ships were important religious and secular symbols. Some graves dating from this period were surrounded by the outline of a ship marked in stones. The cremation of Viking chieftains in their longships has, of course, become a Hollywood cliché. The ship symbol represents the form of travel used by the elder gods who crossed the western ocean to rule Northern Europe in primeval times. Who these gods were, or, indeed, whether they actually existed as mortal human beings, is a speculative question. Esoteric tradition has identified them as the inhabitants of the mythical land of Thule which is said to have existed near Greenland and the Arctic Circle in prehistory (see p. 89).

Mystery surrounds the divine origins of Njord. In the theological struggle which took place between the Aesir and the Vanir it seems possible that the Great Mother Goddess was demoted to a sea god. In the pagan Old Religion the Mother Goddess is traditionally the ruler of the sea which is the womb of all life. The worship of the Nordic Mother Goddess Nerthus took place on an island shrine, and the sea god Njord was also worshipped in temples built on islands off the west coast of Scandinavia. With the confusion surrounding the gods and goddesses of the two rival pantheons, it is quite possible for deities to change sex and adopt the attributes of the preceding divine hierarchy.

Although not recognized as such by the historians of the period, one of the most important, if neglected, deities of the Anglo-Saxon/Germanic pantheon is Weland or Wayland the Smith. He was of giant stock and had the important role of blacksmith to the gods, forging the weapons they used in their battles. Wayland is depicted on the famous Franks casket which illustrates scenes from pagan myth and biblical legend surrounded by runic inscriptions. The casket has been dated as seventh century and is believed to have been manufactured in the north of England. It was named after Sir Alfred Franks who purchased it in the 1860s from a Paris art dealer. This dealer had obtained it from a French farming family who had used it as a sewing work box. On the casket are scenes from the life of Jesus, including the adoration of the Magi. Also featured is Wayland clad in a short kilt which displays the fact that he is lame in one leg. He stands over an anvil with a human head grasped in a pair of tongs. Between his feet lies a decapitated corpse. Two hooded female figures stand facing him. One reaches her arms out towards the smith, while the other holds a basket. To the right of this trio is a woman or boy surrounded by either geese or swans.

Wayland the Smith was the son of the king of Finland. The Finns, as we know, were believed by the ancient Scandinavians to be a race of powerful shamans. He was one of three brothers who became lovers of the Swan Maidens who had flown to a lake near the king's palace. The three Swan Maidens were in fact royal princesses in disguise but after nine years of marriage to the brothers they vanished while their husbands were out hunting. The other two brothers went searching for their errant brides, but Wayland retreated to the marshes near the lake where the Swan Maidens had settled and followed his craft of forging jewellery and weapons.

In time the king of Sweden heard tales of Wayland's wonderful skills and sent armed men to kidnap him. The king made the smith lame so he could not escape and imprisoned him on an island where he was forced to make jewellery for the royal court. One day the king's two sons visited the island and tried to force Wayland into revealing where he had hidden the key to his treasure chest. He told them to return next day and he would tell them exactly what they wanted to know. When the two men eagerly returned the next day Wayland cut off their heads with his magic sword and sent their skulls encrusted with jewels back to the king. Wayland then escaped from the island using a pair of wings he had secretly manufactured during his period of imprisonment.

The story of the divine blacksmith is an ancient one which is also found in Celtic myth. Blacksmiths were regarded as natural magicians because they could tame wild horses and worked with fire and iron. On the Berkshire downs, near the famous White Horse hill figure at Wayland's Smithy, Uffington, stands a prehistoric burial mound surrounded by huge standing stones by the side of an ancient trackway. According to folklore, anyone who leaves a horse by the side of the stones at midnight when the moon is full will return at dawn to find that Wayland has fitted it with new horseshoes. Wayland's ghost is also said to ride out of the mound on winter nights brandishing his magical sword. The link between Wayland and this prehistoric monument suggests that his cult is of great antiquity.

Wayland may also be connected with the dragon or serpent which in Saxon and Scandinavian mythology guards burial mounds and the treasures they contain. When his hiding place within a burial mound is disturbed by grave robbers the dragon responds by chasing the violators and breathing fire. As cremation of the dead was widely practised in ancient times, the dragon may be considered as an elemental spirit of fire. Alternatively, dragons or serpents may have been thought forms created by shaman magicians to guard the mounds. These entities were known in Old English as *wights*, which is a Saxon word denoting a ghost who haunts a graveyard. These spirits were placated by local people with gifts of food left outside the entrances of burial mounds.

In the original pagan myths the serpent or dragon was a symbol of the Earth Goddess, but with the rise of the patriarchal religions which worshipped male sky gods it was transformed into an image of evil and the powers of darkness. In Scandinavian mythology the dragon is the guardian of the Underworld on the Norse sacred tree, which is the realm of departed spirits, elementals, elves and faery folk ruled by the goddesses Hel and Freya.

In addition to the gods of the Aesir, the Vanir and semi-human deities like Wayland the Smith, the Saxon and Norse peoples also paid respect to a host of other minor deities. These included nature spirits representing the elemental power of trees, streams, stones and hills and the pantheon of giants, elves and trolls. Some of the elves were revered as household gods who protected hearth and home from negative influences. Again, as in all forms of pagan spirituality, we find the central concept of divinity manifest in myriad forms. It would be shortsighted for us today, living as we do in a materialistic society which has largely (but not completely) rejected the old gods for atheism or half-hearted Christianity, to regard such a belief system as a primitive one. Pagans certainly believed in a supreme being, but he, she or it revealed itself through the natural world by means of archetypal symbols – the gods and goddesses of ancient myth. The pagan belief in a multiplicity of gods is no more unusual than the modern Catholic's devout acceptance of angels and saints who intercede with God on humankind's behalf.

Although there were many gods and goddesses in the Norse and Germanic religion during the thousand-year period when the use of the runic alphabet was widespread, the main deities seem to have been Odin/Woden, Thor and Frey. Adam of Bremen, writing in the eleventh century CE, states that these three gods were worshipped at the great Swedish sanctuary of Uppsala. He describes the temple in the following words:

These people have a celebrated sanctuary called Uppsala. In this temple, entirely covered with gold, are three idols which the people worship. Thor, as the mightiest god, has his throne in the centre of the hall and Odin and Frey are on either side of him. Thor rules the air, thunder, lightning, storm, rain, fine weather and the crops. Odin is the god of war who inspires men with courage to fight their enemies. Frey gives mankind peace and sensual pleasure. His idol they therefore endow with a mighty phallus. Odin is represented armed in the manner of Mars. Thor is sceptred and resembles Jupiter. Sometimes these people elevate men to the status of deities and endow them with immortality. Attached to the Gods are priests who offer the people's sacrifices. If sickness or famine threaten they offer to the idol Thor, if war to Odin and if a wedding is to be celebrated to Frey. There is a festival at Uppsala every nine years common to all the provinces of Sweden. Attendance at this festival is compulsory and it is the universal practice for both kings and people to send offerings to Uppsala at this time. Those who have become Christians may secure exemption on payment of a fine. The sacrifice on this occasion involves the slaughter of nine males of every creature with whose blood the Gods are placated. The bodies are hung in the precincts of the temple, a sanctuary so holy that each tree is regarded as divine in consequence of the death and decay of the victims. Dogs and horses hang there beside human beings and a Christian has told me that he has seen as many as 72 carcases hanging there side by side. By the way it is said that the songs sung during the ceremony are numerous and obscene so that it is better to say nothing about it.

This is a fascinating account by a contemporary chronicler and contains several interesting facts about pagan life in Scandinavia. First, Adam was writing in the eleventh century and it is obvious that paganism was still very much the common practice in Sweden. Most other European countries had been converted to the new faith for several centuries when his graphic account of pagan worship was written. A certain amount of pagan tolerance was shown to those practising Christians who did not wish to attend the rites held at Uppsala every nine years. If the roles had been reversed there is no doubt that the pagans would have been forced to attend whether they agreed or not. This shows a more enlightened attitude towards Christianity than was practised by those Christians who encountered pagan beliefs and practices. It is true that at first the Christian missionaries ignored the survival of pagan customs, but as they grew more powerful politically they began to persecute anyone who dared follow the Old Ways. In Adam of Bremen's time the balance was changing towards the Church and it was beginning to harden its attitude towards the Old Religion.

Another interesting point is the statement that the pagans sometimes deified men of outstanding ability after their death. If this was a common practice in pagan Northern Europe, then could a wandering shaman called Odin who invented a magical alphabet have been made a god when he died? It is a tantalizing thought.

The special festival held at Uppsala every nine years suggests a symbolic link with the Yggdrasil tree and the nine worlds of Norse myth. Nine was a sacred number to the Scandinavians. It is a lunar number representing the three phases of the moon (symbolizing the Triple Goddess) multiplied by itself. The lore of this sacred number belongs to an older religious tradition than the worship of either Odin or Thor. It suggests a throwback to the divine ancestors of the Vanir cult who were worshipped in pre-Aryan times.

We may shudder at the gruesome description of public sacrifices held at the Swedish temple. Although blood sacrifice was widely practised in pagan societies, it had become debased. In any consideration of the alleged sacrificial rites performed at Uppsala we should first examine the background to the story related by Adam of Bremen. He was writing from a Christian viewpoint and at the time he penned his account the Church's view of paganism was changing rapidly. Within two hundred years it was to launch its crusade against heretics within the Church and shortly afterwards turned its attention to the surviving followers of the pagan faith who were ruthlessly exterminated in the witch hunts. Although blood sacrifice was practised in the Jewish religion, it does not feature in the published sayings of Jesus and there is no evidence that it was practised by the early Christians, either Jews or Gentiles.

The evidence for the extensive carnage at the festival in Uppsala originates from a Christian informant who was an eyewitness to the ritual killings. In accepting Adam's evidence we must ask ourselves if it is likely that a practising Christian would have been allowed near the pagan shrine at such a time. With their fear and hatred of the pagan beliefs, it also seems very unlikely that any Christians of the period would disguise their true religious persuasion and gatecrash such a ceremony. In its attempt to denigrate the pagan Old Religion and establish its own form of spiritual totalitarianism in medieval Europe, the Church used many forms of false propaganda.

Norse and Saxon pagans celebrated many different religious festivals throughout the year, following a ritualized pattern of worship. According to Bede, the pagan Anglo-Saxons began their year on 25 December with a festival known as the Night of the Mothers. It is speculation whether this night celebrated human mothers or the Great Goddess. The latter seems more likely. The festival coincides with Yule (Old Norse *jol* or Old English *geol* meaning 'wheel'), which was celebrated at the winter solstice and has now become our modern Christmas. As its name suggests, this was the time of the year when the wheel of life turned and there was a pause between the old year dying and the new year being born. Today, with increased holidays over the Christmas period, the ancient celebration of the twelve days of Yuletide is once more becoming a reality.

The season from Winter's Night or Hallowe'en (31 October) and the winter solstice was traditionally when the Wild Hunt led by Odin or his Celtic counterpart Cernunnos rode the night sky. Odin has been equated with Father Christmas who rides across the sky with his reindeer sledge and hands out gifts as the hooded god did at this season. Father Christmas is a pagan figure despite his dubious links with Saint Nicholas. There are many other pagan symbols which feature in the festive season, including the Christmas tree which is traditionally a fir.

The candles on the tree represent the planets and their ruling pagan gods. On top of the tree is either a fairy doll, representing the Great Goddess, or a star symbolizing the Pole Star. This stellar object was known to the Germanic tribes as 'the nail star'. This was because it was believed to be the nail which held the heavens to their point of support. To the pagan people of Scandinavia the north was a sacred point of the compass. It was the place where the elder gods lived, according to Norse mythology. When the Church tried to encourage the pagans to accept the east as the new sacred direction, it came across strong opposition. In Nordic myth the east was the home of the Fenris Wolf and the frost giants who were in conflict with the Aesir.

To the pagan Scandinavians Yule was a celebration to mark the lowest point of the sun in the sky and its rising again towards the spring tide. As well as being a joyous time of merry-making, Yule was also the time for taking vows which had to be kept during the coming year. This pagan practice has survived today in our modern observance of New Year resolutions. The old medieval custom of a boar's head being placed on the Christmas table with an apple in its mouth dates from Norse Yule rites to Frey. The boar was Frey's sacred animal and was sacrificed as an offering at New Year to ensure a fruitful twelve months.

The main festivals of the Norse ritual year (and also of the Saxons', who followed a very similar pattern) were as follows:

Norse	Roman	Festival	Date (approx.)
Wolfmoon	December	Yule	21st/22nd
		Night of the Mothers	25th
Snowmoon	January	Blessing the Plough	6th
Horningmoon	February	Festival of the Family	14th
Lentingmoon	March	Summer Finding (Spring equinox)	21st
Ostaramoon	April	Eostre	Full moon
Merrymoon	May	May Day	1st
Fallowmoon	June-July	Midsummer	21 June
Harvestmoon	August	Harvest Festival	31st
Sheddingmoon	September	Winter Finding (Autumn equinox)	21st
Huntingmoon	October	Winter's Night	31st
Fogmoon	November	Fallen Heroes' Day	11th

Like so many other pagan calendars, the Norse/Saxon one follows a lunar cycle. In fact, our modern word 'month' is derived from 'moon', and in common parlance we sometimes speak of 'many moons'. We do so without realizing its original significance as a time division associated with the matrifocal worship of the Great Goddess.

We have already mentioned some of these festivals earlier in the book. They are linked with the seasonal changes and the agricultural year, which is exactly what one would expect from a pastoral people with a rural-based economy. Some of these festivals were Christianized by the Church in its early attempts to eradicate its pagan rivals. It soon realized that it was impossible totally to destroy paganism, so the Church took the soft option of taking over the ancient festivals and rededicating them to Christian saints. Pagan temples were demolished and churches built on their sites in the hope that the pagans would still come to their old sacred places but to worship the new god.

The pagan festival of the Family on 14 February coincides with both the Christianized St Valentine's Day and the Feast of the Lupercalia – on 15 February – in the old Roman calendar. On that date the young men of Rome ran through the streets clad in wolves' pelts chasing naked women. Anyone unlucky enough to be caught by the wolf men was beaten with scourges. Flagellation in ancient cultures was regarded as a fertility rite not a perverse sexual practice as it is today in our permissive society.

Easter, which is the major Christian festival of death and rebirth, derives its name from Eostre, the Saxon goddess of the dawn and springtime. She is associated with the Daeg Rune and was worshipped at the spring equinox. The traditional Easter eggs represent fertility, and the Easter bunny is the hare which was sacred to both Celts and Norse pagans as a symbol of the Great Goddess. Even hot-cross buns have a pagan significance, for the symbol which gives them their name is not the unbalanced cross of Christianity but the equal-armed solar cross of the Old Faith.

Midsummer was Christianized as St John's Day but is still widely celebrated in Scandinavia, Germany and Finland with pagan bonfires, ring dancing and the erection of phallic Maypoles. In the Swedish-speaking areas of Finland the Maypole or Majstang is decorated with wild flowers and leaves and is thought to bring good fortune to crops, humans and animals. In the nineteenth century Finnish country folk practised magical spells at Midsummer to increase the fertility of their animals. One of these folk spells involved the placing of a wreath of wild flowers around the neck of each cow and muttering secret incantations. This was said to increase the milk yield.

The safe gathering in of the harvest was recognized at the end of

August with rites to Frey, while the oncoming of winter ruled by the cosmic power of ice was observed at the autumn equinox at the end of September. This festival was Christianized as Michaelmas and since the nineteenth century the Church has practised its own Harvest Festival around this time. Winter Night on 31 October is the modern Hallowe'en or All Souls' Eve when witches and ghosts are said to ride the night sky with the Wild Hunt. This is the time for trick-or-treat, apple bobbing and candles spluttering in pumpkin masks. Finally, on 11 November is Fallen Heroes' Day, which coincides with our modern Armistice ceremony to remember the dead of two world wars.

As well as these folk memories of the ancient Norse and Saxon pagan festivals, the names of the Nordic gods survive in our modern days of the week as follows:

Day of the week	God/Goddess	Planet	Rulership
Monday	Freya	Moon	Psychic powers
Tuesday	Tiw	Mars	Strength
Wednesday	Woden/Odin	Mercury	Wisdom and knowledge
Thursday	Thor	Jupiter	Material wealth
Friday	Frigga	Venus	Sexuality
Saturday	The Norns	Saturn	Fate
Sunday	Baldur/Frey	Sun	Fertility and healing

It is through the naming of the days of the weeks after the Nordic gods and goddesses and the Christianization of the old pagan festivals that the lore of the Rune system has survived. There can be no real comprehension of the Runes without an understanding of their position in relation to the pagan North European religion. Each Rune is an archetypal symbol relating to the spiritual and philosophical concepts believed in by the pagan Scandinavians and Germans. Only by a close study of the spiritual symbolism of the runic alphabet will the seeker learn to appreciate the Ancient Wisdom which it represents.

9

In our examination of the Rune symbols we have placed considerable emphasis on their role as guideposts on the spiritual path. Each Rune is a pictographic symbol and has a number of meanings on both the material and spiritual level. In a philosophical model it would be incorrect to depict these levels as existing separately or one above the other. The teaching encapsulated in the Rune system is firmly based on the pagan premise that spirit and matter are one. It was not until medieval Christianity was established that the false idea arose that the natural world was evil and sinful. This belief seems to have been inherited from the Persian doctrine of Zoroastrianism which taught that the universe was a cosmic battleground between the powers of light and darkness. Such ideas percolated into medieval Christian theology through various heresies which received considerable support among the peasant population of France in the twelfth and thirteenth centuries. The dichotomy between matter and spirit was further reinforced in the Age of Reason by the rise of scientific intellectualism as preached by humanist philosophers such as Réné Descartes. He taught a new religion based on materialism and the self consciousness of human beings to guide their own destiny.

It is possible that the Norse and Germanic mythologies may have been influenced by the teachings of Zoroaster as they sprang from common Indo-European roots. The battle between the forces of good and evil as represented by Baldur and Loki and the final conflict of Ragnarok suggest that this may have been the case. However, the extreme vision of good and evil presented by Christian theologians in the Middle Ages would not have been recognized by most pagans of the Rune period. However evil the opposing forces in the cosmic struggle may appear in the myths woven around them, the pagan view was that ultimately both good and evil are aspects of the same reality.

When we deal with the spiritual quest represented by the runic system we find a practical approach to the attainment of enlightenment. The shamanistic path offers contact with the gods, the spirits of the dead and the Otherworld. The emphasis in the spiritual meanings of the Runes is that the spirit shines through the apparent dross of material existence. In the Eastern religions the ultimate aim of the mystic is to escape from the wheel of life, death and rebirth and to be absorbed into the eternal. The ordinary reality of the material world is regarded as *maya* or illusion. In the teachings of Islam and Christianity the faithful are promised a reward in the afterlife for good behaviour (by the standards of the priesthood) and adherence to a strict moral code during incarnation in the material world. In the pagan cosmic view which is exemplified in the Celtic, Norse and Saxon versions of the Old Religion, the material or natural world is not rejected as either an illusion or a temptation to be resisted. The gods, nature spirits and the fallen heroes co-exist with mortals within the realm of the physical plane. Nature is divine, the old gods live in the hollow hills and Odin walks the highways and byways of Middle Earth in human guise. Even Asgard, the realm of the gods, is joined to Middle Earth and the Underworld by the Rainbow Bridge. The symbolism of the pagan Old Religion is not based on abstract philosophical concepts but is firmly rooted in the natural things which exist around us. Indeed, the personifications of natural forces represented by the gods are merely different aspects of All-That-Is which is the life force made manifest through the universe.

This fact is graphically illustrated by the symbolic images associated with each of the runic characters. They include cattle, a thorn, a blazing torch, hail, ice, a yew tree, sedgegrass, the sun, a birch tree, a horse, water, dawn, the ancestral home. These are commonplace symbols which each of us can encounter on a daily basis if we have any awareness of our surroundings. Through the use of these material metaphors the Rune Masters weaved a potent spiritual spell explaining metaphysical concepts which otherwise would have been difficult for ordinary people to grasp. Jesus understood this process for he revealed the inner teachings of his native Judaic religion by proverbs and parables.

The path followed by the initiate of the Northern European mysteries leads towards a form of spiritual enlightenment. An individual's understanding of what this experience means depends largely on his racial, cultural and religious outlook. A superficial analysis of the pagans' lifestyle has led some critics to dismiss them as hedonistic materialists. However, their spirituality is very similiar to the inner teachings of many comparative religions. They share a deep-rooted belief in the oneness of all life, a belief that the power or force we call God is a representation of the totality of spiritual and material existence. The goal of the seeker on the spiritual path is to become one with God. This is to experience, even only for a fraction of a second, total awareness of the cosmic unity. On the way to this ultimate goal the seeker learns some valuable lessons concerning conduct towards the other life forms sharing Middle Earth and the way in which humankind and the gods – who are symbolic images of the unity – interact to create the cosmic pattern we know as reality. This cosmic pattern can be recognized in the changing seasons and the different stages in the life of the seeker as he or she gradually develops in character and personality.

The division between the use of the Runes as a divinatory tool and their wider application as archetypal keys for unlocking spiritual potential at first seems very wide to the person encountering them for the purpose of predicting the future. However, just as the Tao is the spiritual philosophy behind the I Ching, so the Runes are supported by the cosmic overview of the Norse and Teutonic religious perspective. Central to the Runes as a method of accurate divination is the Wyrd. This power, which has been compared to the Western idea of Fate and the Eastern belief in Karma, provides a metaphysical basis for the use of the runic alphabet both as an aid to divination and as a spiritual blueprint for self-development.

In our modern consumer society it is difficult to imagine the hardship of life in medieval times. It cannot be denied that the average middle-class person living today would find life difficult if transported back through time to the Viking Age. In a society based on agriculture which did not possess the benefits of EEC subsidies or mass chemicalization if the crops failed, the tribe could be faced with a major disaster. It is human nature to look around for a scapegoat on which to blame such events. An element of this attitude permeates Northern European paganism, but generally such negative experiences were regarded as tests by the gods and were explained by the power of the Wyrd.

One translation of the word 'Wyrd' renders it as 'experience' or 'trial', although it was used collectively to denote the powers of destiny or fate. Originally the Wyrd was regarded as a separate goddess who used to spin the fate of humanity like threads on a spinning wheel. The image of the goddess who weaves the web of destiny was common in the classical period. It seems to have been derived from the Indo-European religious tradition which formed the basis of the Greek, Roman, Celtic, Saxon and Norse religions. In Greek mythology, for instance, the three Morai or Fates were spinners. One of the goddesses spun the thread of life (birth), another measured the thread (life), while the third cut the thread (death). In Old English the key words of 'weave', 'destiny' and 'fortune' were often associated with each other, which suggests an occult meaning.

In Norse mythology the power of the Wyrd was symbolized by the Norns, the triad of goddess figures who dwelt on the sacred World Tree. They were called Urdr (Fate), Verdani (Being) and Skuld (Necessity). Every day they took water from a sacred spring, mixed it with earth and anointed the roots of the tree to prevent it rotting away. This symbolic act represents the immense power of the Wyrd to protect and sustain the cosmic order. Like Freya, the Norns are another aspect of the Triple Goddess who appears as the Maiden, Mother and Crone. Urdr is an old woman who looks backwards over her shoulder to the past. Verdani is a young girl who gazes forward at the present. Skuld is veiled and sits on a chair with an unopened scroll on her lap. She represents the future which, under normal circumstances, is a closed book.

The Norns were attended by a company of young women who materialized in dreams to impart guidance and advice to mortals. These Norn maidens were also given the task by their mistresses of finding pregnant women for the souls of the discarnate to be born to. As personifications of the Wyrd, it is only right they should claim province over the forces of life and death.

With the coming of the new religion, the Wyrd refused to be disregarded and survived for some time after the conversion of the pagan tribes. At first the early Church accepted the Wyrd as an aspect of God until it became theologically uncomfortable. It was obvious that a power of destiny or fate which was associated by the pagans with a triplicity of goddesses could not easily be accepted into mainstream Christian belief. If the Christian God was, as his worshippers claimed, the supreme being and there were no other gods, the existence of a separate divine force known as the Wyrd was difficult to explain. Although the Holy Trinity and the Devil had been accepted into the early Christian teachings, suggesting that God was not omnipotent, there was no place for the Wyrd.

Belief in the Wyrd survived among the common people who, unlike the upper social classes in early medieval Europe, still practised paganism despite lipservice to the new faith. In the eleventh century a prominent cleric in Worms had to rebuke peasant women because they believed in three female spirits who could influence the lives of their unborn babies. Pregnant women even laid extra places at their tables for these divine visitors. A Danish king took his young son to see three sybils who lived in a cave and are obviously disguised versions of the Norns. The first sybil granted the boy the gift of charm, the second granted him generosity, but the third decreed that he should be prudent in the exercise of these abilities.

Despite their suppression by the Church, the Norns emerged in some odd forms in folk culture. They appear as the fairy godmothers, equipped with a spinning wheel, who materialize at the birth of royal children. In the fairy tales of *Sleeping Beauty* and *Snow White and the Seven Dwarves* the Norns become wicked stepmothers. The fairy tales which we read to our children today conceal pagan symbols which survived in popular folk literature long after they had ceased to have any religious meaning in contemporary society.

Perhaps the most dramatic example of the Norns re-emerging from the collective unconscious as archetypal images is their appearance as the three witches in William Shakespeare's classic play *Macbeth*. Shakespeare, or whoever wrote the plays attributed to him, was well versed in the occult and the popular folk beliefs of Elizabethan England. He also seems to have had a considerable knowledge of classical paganism. His witches in *Macbeth* do not call upon the Devil as they squat around the cauldron on the blasted heath, but invoke the three-faced Greek goddess Hecate. In a period when the accepted image of witches was as Satanic devil worshippers, this radical interpretation of the sisterhood as followers of the pagan Old Religion must have caused some surprise among the theatregoers who flocked to see the play.

Shakespeare calls his three witches the Weird Sisters. The Old English word 'weird' is derived from the root *wyrd*. In the *Oxford English Dictionary* the word weird is listed under two separate headings. The first designates it to mean 'fate' or 'destiny'. The second refers to its connection with fate but also gives the secondary meanings of 'supernatural', 'uncanny', 'strange' or 'incomprehensible'. This 'otherness' of its second meanings links the word with the old pagan belief in the power of Fate. By naming his witches the Weird Sisters, the Elizabethan playwright was telling anyone who knew anything about pre-Christian myths that they were the Norns in human form.

In *Macbeth* the three Weird Sisters are credited with the supernatural power to foretell the future. It is evident from their spells and their cryptic comments to the Scottish noble that they are also able to control the forces of destiny. This again connects the witches with the Norns. It is interesting to speculate that the theatrical superstition that

Macbeth is an unlucky play originated in the ancient belief in the awesome power of the Wyrd to affect the lives of mortals.

Attempts have been made to align the Wyrd with the Eastern concept of Karma. This term has become commonplace nowadays with the influx of oriental religious ideas into the West. Karma is derived from a Sanscrit word meaning 'action', and refers to our attitudes and actions while incarnate on Middle Earth. In the Hindu and Buddhist belief in reincarnation it is accepted that any future lives we may have will be determined by our deeds in our present incarnation. On a simplistic level, the workings of Karma can be summarized in the Jewish edict of 'An eye for an eye and a tooth for a tooth'. In theory, if we commit a bad act in this life we will suffer for it in some future, as yet undetermined, life. In the Eastern religions it is quite conceivable for humans to be reborn as animals in their next existence if they have broken the moral code.

In practice, the workings of Karma are much more subtle than this, but the acceptance of punishment in a future life for transgression in this one features strongly. The way that punishment is meted out is the point where Eastern and Western interpretations of Karma tend to separate. Like all esoteric truths which have been adopted through mass communication for general public consumption, the concept of Karma has become debased. In its original form it teaches that we are not isolated from each other as individuals existing within our own private world, but that each of us can affect those around us.

We are all threads in the web of life woven by the Wyrd. There are pyschics who have tuned in to natural disasters and who describe the experience as 'the web trembling'. As John Donne said, no man is an island; we must accept our responsibility for all the other life forms which share Middle Earth with us. This vision of moral responsibility has been espoused by modern ecologists but it already featured in the pagan spirituality which was the foundation of the ancient Rune system.

During the last few hundred years humanity has gradually withdrawn from the natural world. Today millions of people live in concrete jungles, surviving on processed junk food and being entertained by electronic gimmickry, and have no real contact with nature. This abnormal state would have been regarded with horror by the ancient tribal people who lived, as far as is possible in an agricultural society, in harmony with nature. With this ultra-materialism came the scientific belief that human beings were conditioned to behave in certain ways because of hereditary traits, past experiences or their reaction to the environment around them. Fate, destiny or the Wyrd obviously has no role to play in such a dehumanized and mechanical philosophy of material existence.

This nihilistic attitude can be compared with the role that the Wyrd played in pagan Scandinavian and Saxon life. During the Viking Age the Indo-European image of the warrior became a powerful cultural archetype. The noble virtues of the individual were elevated to a position in society which may seem to be extreme in our own collective culture. The pagan notions of honour, discipline, self-reliance and courage attracted many disillusioned Germans after the First World War and laid the moral foundation for the rise of Fascism. However, it would be wrong to think that the positive cultivation of these virtues results in the automatic adoption of a reactionary and authoritarian social outlook as illustrated by the political situation in Germany from 1933. It should be remembered that these social values were exercised in Norse and German society within an extended family unit. In practice this meant that the individual, while possessing a considerable degree of personal freedom of action, was also responsible for the other members of the tribe. Indeed, the continued survival of the tribe depended upon this form of social responsibility being closely followed. This included loyalty to friends, catering to the needs of the young, the infirm and the old, and the upholding of a 'caring society' within the tribal context.

The high moral principles which governed the society who used the Runes can be summarized as follows. First, trust and devotion in the sphere of friendship and social contact. The pagan Norsefolk believed that if a friendship turned sour, or for some reason a trusted friend turned against you, then the new situation should be accepted philosophically. It should be recognized that even the closest friendships experience periods of unrest. If a friendship is destined to last, then it will survive such a period and emerge in a stronger form. Oath taking was an important aspect of Viking society and anyone who broke an oath was treated as a social outcast. This was doubly so if the oath had been sworn before the gods on the altar of a pagan sanctuary. The person who betrayed the sacred oath had to face the terrible consequences of his action and deal with his Wyrd alone, without help from other members of the tribe.

Tribal laws decreed that the old should be treated with respect. Although contact with outsiders for trade was essential to the prosperity of society, the Norse social code taught them to be friendly to strangers but not to put too much trust in their pledges. This rather chauvinistic attitude was based on the belief that, however enlightened outsiders might be, when it came down to basics their attitudes and social customs were different.

In a Norse poem known as *Havamal* or *The Sayings of the High One* and attributed to Odin there are several axioms which reflect the general attitude of the pagan Scandinavians. Here is a selection which gives a flavour of the Norse morality in practice.

When a guest arrives chilled to the knees from his journey through the hills he needs fire, food and dry clothes.

A man must be reticent, thoughtful and bold in battle. Cheerful and active until death.

A coward thinks he will live for ever if he avoids his enemies but old age escapes no man even if he survives the spears.

A visitor must leave in time and not overstay his welcome. Even a friend becomes odious if he bides too long in the house of his host.

To one's friend one must be a friend and to his friend. But to one's enemy's friend no man should be a friend.

A man must be moderately wise, never too wise. The man whose mind is most free of care does not know his fate in advance.

A lame man can ride a horse. A man without land can be a shepherd. A deaf man can kill. It is better to be blind than burned on the funeral pyre. A dead man is of no use to anyone.

No man is so good as to be free of all evil. Nor so bad as to be worth nothing.

Never confide your troubles to a bad man. He will never repay with good your open-heartedness.

Never quarrel with a fool. A wise man will often refrain from fighting whereas a fool will fight without cause or reason.

Do not break an alliance with a friend. Your heart will grieve if you lose the friend in whom you confide.

Cattle die, kinsmen die, I myself shall die. But there is one thing that never dies – the reputation we leave behind at death.

We can see from the above axioms that the pagan Norsefolk believed in living life to the full. They believed it was better to be physically handicapped than dead. They put great value on friendship but even the closest friend could outstay his welcome.

Such values offer a blueprint for the seeker following the path of the

Northern European mystery tradition. The emphasis on self-reliance, free will and the assertion of the individual on both spiritual and material levels are the essential keynotes. As the seeker progresses through the lessons taught by each of the runic symbols he or she learns a different aspect of right living. Each Rune represents a step in the direction of self-awareness of the seeker's position in the cosmos.

The real source of the Ancient Wisdom of the Runes is shrouded in mystery. In our study of their historical origins it is surmised that the Runes may have originated in northern Italy and been carried by wandering shamans to Germany and Scandinavia. The mystical homeland of the runic tradition in neo-Germanic esotericism is the legendary land of Thule. This huge island, situated somewhere between Scandinavia, Britain, Greenland and the Arctic Circle, was destroyed in a natural disaster thousands of years ago.

The famous description by Hecataeus in 500 BCE of a legendary Hyperborean land has been identified by Celtic writers with the British Isles, but it is more likely that he was describing the lost continent of Thule.

In the region beyond the land of the Celti there lies in the ocean an island no smaller than Sicily. This island is situated in the north and is inhabited by the Hyperboreans who are called by that name because they are beyond the point where the north wind blows. This island is fertile and productive of every crop and since it has an unusually temperate climate it produces two harvests a year. Apollo is the god honoured above all gods and the inhabitants are looked upon as the priests of Apollo since daily they praise the god in song and honour him exceedingly. And there is also on the island both a magnificent sacred precinct of Apollo and a notable temple which is adorned with many votive offerings and is built after the pattern of the spheres.

According to Hecataeus' account, the Hyperboreans had their own special language but were friendly towards the Greeks who 'inherited their goodwill from ancient times'. The god called Apollo can be identified as the sun/sky god of the Bronze Age Scandinavians. It seems likely that both the Hyperboreans and the Greeks had a shared cultural and racial origin.

The most detailed argument for a connection between the legends of lost Atlantis and Thule have been made by an Austrian priest called Jurgen Spanuth. In 1953, following archaeological excavations he made in Heligoland, Spanuth published his controversial book *Atlantis Revealed* in which he claimed that the lost land was a Northern European country. He followed this up with a second book, *Atlantis of the North*, published in 1979, which he regarded as providing absolute proof of his theory.

The generally held belief about Atlantis is that it was an island continent in the Atlantic ocean between Africa and South America. It was destroyed by divine intervention because of the corrupt practices of its people. This destruction spanned a number of years and involved volcanic eruptions, tidal waves and earthquakes. According to occult tradition, the Atlanteans practised black magic, worshipped idols of their kings as gods, mated with animals to create a subhuman race and misused technology for evil purposes. Shortly before the final destruction of the island a small group of Atlantean adepts fled their ravaged homeland. They colonized remote parts of South America, Northern Africa and Western Europe and elements of their culture and religion were adopted by the aboriginal inhabitants of these places.

The only historical evidence for Atlantis is the story which the Greek philosopher and statesman Solon brought back from Egypt in the sixth century BCE. This story was derived from records preserved inside an Egyptian temple. The Egyptian priests translated the inscriptions for Solon because they told of a major battle between the Atlanteans and the ancient Greeks. According to the priests, this battle had occured some 9000 years earlier.

Most scholars who have attempted to prove that Atlantis existed outside of myth and legend have dismissed the story of the Atlantean conquest of Greece as a fairy tale. Spanuth in his controversial theory dates Atlantis's maximum period of influence as 1200 BCE. He cites evidence that during the reign of Pharaoh Ramses III North Africa was invaded by a mysterious Sea People from the north who wore horned helmets. He identifies these warriors from the sea as the inhabitants of Thule/Atlantis. According to the papyri recording this event, the Sea People came from 'the islands and coastlands of the ocean in the farthest north'. Friendly relationships seemed to have been established with the Sea People for in the reign of Tutmoses III an emissary from 'the northern land from the far ends of the Earth' brought the pharaoh a gift of amber. We know that amber was sacred to the Great Goddess in pagan Scandinavia and during the Bronze Age was exported from that area all over Europe.

Atlantis was named after the giant in Greek mythology who supported the heavens on his shoulders. Spanuth points out that the ancient Greeks believed that Atlas lived in the land of the Hyperboreans in the north. According to the same Greek sources, the land of the Hyperboreans lay in the Atlantic ocean near the land of the

Celts. In *The Eddas* Scandinavia is referred to as Atland from the name of an ancient king who once ruled over all the northern lands.

Spanuth believes that the Atlanteans known historically as the Sea People occupied many parts of the Mediterranean including Cyprus and Greece. He cites the discovery in Cyprus of Germanic hilted swords and the bronze statue of a man wearing what looks like a knitted cap from which protrude bull's horns. This figurine represents the so-called 'horned Apollo', who was introduced by the Sea People into the Mediterranean. This deity was a representation of the Indo-European sky god who wore horns.

The theory about a northern Atlantis must remain mere speculation despite the circumstantial evidence in its favour. To date, there has been no geological evidence offered for the existence of either Thule or Atlantis. The concept of an ancient lost continent inhabited by godlike beings has captured the imagination of many occultists and psychics who have dabbled in Runecraft or the Norse religion. It held a fascination for several leading members of the German National Socialist Party during the period between 1933 and 1945 when they sought to pervert the Northern European mysteries for their dark political purposes. It has been suggested that the German Socialist Workers Party, which included Hitler as one of its early members, was the political wing of a magical group known as the Thule Gessellschaft. This secret group of anti-Semitic German occultists combined a belief in the existence of the lost island of Thule with the study of Runelore, Norse religion and the Aryan master race.

On their sudden rise to power certain members of the GNSP attempted to reconstruct the Norse beliefs as a form of state religion. Their interest in the ancient Nordic religious practices was linked with their false belief that the Aryans or Indo-Europeans were superior to all other races, especially the Jews, gypsies and coloureds. Hitler and his fanatical associates could not accept Christianity because of its Jewish background so they attempted to found a new pagan religion based on the worship of the Norse gods. In their rejection of all aspects of Judeo-Christianity they even searched for a new scientific theory which would explain the creation of the universe. They found what they were looking for in the bizarre ideas of an Austrian businessman called Hans Hoerbiger.

While at work Hoerbiger had had a mystical experience which changed his life. Watching an explosion created by molten metal falling on frozen mud, he formulated his World Ice Theory which he preached until his death in 1931. High-ranking officers in the GNSP who were interesting in reviving the Norse religion seized upon Hoerbiger's theory because it offered a quasi-scientific theory of the universe which paralleled the creation myth of the pagan Scandinavians.

Hoerbiger believed that millions of years ago a super star collided in galactic space with a huge mass of solid ice. From the resulting explosion pieces of ice were hurled across space and created the planets of our solar system. Surrounding the solar system is a gigantic ring of ice which is believed, falsely, by astronomers to be the Milky Way. Each planet of solidified ice circles the sun – the centre of fire – until eventually it will collide with it and be destroyed. From this meeting of fire and ice a new planetary system will be formed.

According to Hoerbiger, the earth once possessed three moons which preceded our present one. Each of these moons had crashed into the earth at different periods of history, destroying the ancient civilizations which existed at the line. He divided the history of Middle Earth into four cosmic ages, each ruled by one of the moons. The first age was one of primitive vegetation and insects, the second age was of the dinosaurs, the third age was that of Atlantis and Thule, and the fourth age is that of our modern civilization.

Hoerbiger believed that our present moon was moving closer to the planet and because of this its cosmic influence was growing stronger, leading to spiritual awareness and the birth of a new race of superhuman beings who would become the rulers of the next civilization. The fanatical GNSP members who accepted Hoerbiger's theories as fact identified this new super-race with the pure-blooded Aryans who they believed were survivors of the destruction of the lost land of Thule. Let us hope that none of the people who study the Runes today are drawn to the insanity represented by Hitler and his followers.

Although the theories of Hoerbiger and the GNSP must be rejected out of hand, the idea of Thule and its shamanistic priesthood of magical adepts as the spiritual homeland of the runic wisdom remains a potent image. There are those who believe that the Ancient Wisdom which lies at the Runes' centre originated from a mythical source. Others believe that the Hyperborean land of Thule was a historical reality and that shortly before its destruction certain shamans were chosen to leave the island. They travelled across Europe to Asia and became the ancestors of the Indo-Europeans. Several thousand years later their descendants made the journey back across Europe searching, if only unconsciously, for their mystical homeland now submerged beneath the waves.

Such a theory is attractive to those who believe that before the rise of the great Middle Eastern civilizations there existed a pan-European culture which was their equal. While the actual reality of Thule must remain a historical enigma, the Ancient Wisdom of the Runes offers a powerful testimony to the past existence of a body of arcane knowledge which is the spiritual heritage of our present culture.

If we are spiritually to rediscover our racial roots and re-establish the pagan values of our ancestors which are relevant to our present planetary crisis, then we must look back into the past to the golden age represented by the myth of Thule. It will act as a focus for the liberation of those ancient spiritual energies which, once released from the European collective unconscious, will illuminate Middle Earth.

Glossary of Norse/Germanic Mythological and Religious Terminology

Aesir   The dynasty of Indo-European sky gods

Alcis   The twin gods worshipped by the ancient Germani

Alfar   Household elves or gods said to protect the home from negative influences

Amanita muscaria   The latin name for fly agaric, the red-capped toadstool or sacred mushroom used as a natural narcotic in rites to Odin and in Runecasting

Asgard   The mythological home of the Norse gods

Auohumla (trans. rich horned cow)   Primeval archetypal cow which nourished Ymir in the Norse creation myth

Baldur   The beautiful young sun god ritually slain by Holdur

Berserkers   Warrior priests of Odin who, intoxicated on mead or sacred mushrooms, were possessed by battle fury

Bifrost   The Norse name for the Rainbow Bridge that linked Asgard with Middle Earth

Blot   A sacrificial feast

Disir   Female spirits or goddesses who attended Freya

Flyfot   The Anglo-Saxon name for the swastika

Fenris   The giant wolf who was bound by the gods with the aid of Tyr

Frey   The ithyphallic god of fertility

Freya   The Scandinavian goddess of fertility, childbirth, psychism and death

Frigga   The wife of Odin and goddess of sexual love

Futhark   The Germanic term for the runic alphabet

Galdr   Sacred songs or magical incantations

Godhi   A priest of the Norse Old Religion

Havamal (trans. 'Sayings of the Old One')   An epic Norse poem credited to Odin

Heimdall   The guardian god of the Rainbow Bridge

Hel   The daughter of Loki and Queen of the Underworld

Hodur   The blind god who slew Baldur

Ing   The Saxon fertility god said to be a version of Frey

Irminsul   The sacred World Tree or pillar supporting the heavens in Germanic myth

Loki   The Norse god of fire

Mead   A drink made of honey and apples used as intoxicant in rites to Odin

Midgard (trans. Middle Earth)   The material world of humankind

Mimir   The Norse god of wisdom

Mjollnir   Thor's magical hammer

Nerthus   The early Germanic Great Mother Goddess

Niflheim   The place of darkness on the sacred World Tree

Nine worlds   The nine heavens or nine planes of existence in Norse cosmology

Njord   The Norse sea god

Norns   Three goddesses who weave the web of destiny and represent the power of the Wyrd

Odin   The one-eyed, hooded god of the Runes

Ragnarok (trans. Destruction of the Powers)   The final conflict between the Gods, the Fenris Wolf and the frost giants that leads to a new cosmic order

Rune Master or **Rune Mistress**   A person skilled in the use of the Runes for divination or for magical workings

Skald   A Norse poet; is equivalent to a Celtic bard

Sleipnir   Odin's eight-legged horse

Thor   The Norse thunder god

Troll   In Norse folklore, a Goblin-like creature living underground

Tyr, Tiw   The Norse god of war

Valhalla (trans. Hall of the Slain)   The place where the souls of dead warriors are taken after death

Valkryies (trans. Choosers of the Slain)   Female spirits who collect the souls of dead warriors from the battlefield and carry them to Valhalla

Vanir   The pre-Aryan dynasty of fertility gods and goddesses

VE (trans. sacred or holy place)   A pagan sanctuary or temple

Volva   A seeress

Wayland   The smith of the gods

Wiccae   The Anglo-Saxon term for witchcraft, i.e. the post-Christian survival of the pagan Old Religion

Wizard   (trans. wise man)   Medieval term for a male witch or magician

Ymir   Hermaphrodite giant who gave birth to the first man and woman in the Norse creation myth.

Chronology

35,000–8000 BCE	Old Stone Age	Worship of Great Mother Goddess. Shamanism
8000–5000 BCE	New Stone Age	Fertility cults with gods and goddesses. Ancestor Worship. Hunting magic
5000–2000 BCE	Early Bronze Age	Earliest recorded writing. Fertility cults worshipping Great Mother Goddess and her male consorts. Stone circles and other megalithic monuments erected
2000–1000 BCE	Late Bronze Age	Stonehenge built. Sun worship in Northern Europe; votive offerings in peat bogs
1000–500 BCE	Early Iron Age	Rise of Celtic and early Nordic civilizations with worship of deified heroes and fertility gods and goddesses
500 BCE–100 CE	Late Iron Age	Use of the runic alphabet. Human sacrifices in the Scandinavian peat bogs. Emergence of Odinism
100–500 CE	The Roman Age	Roman occupation of Western Europe. The worship of Norse and Germanic gods. Early Christianity emerges
500–1000 CE	Early Middle Ages	Rise of Viking and Saxon cultures. Period of dual faith with paganism and Christianity in conflict
1000–1500 CE	Late Middle Ages	Suppression of paganism

Bibliography

Bede, *A History of the English Church and People* (Penguin, 1955)

Brian Branston, *The Lost Gods of England* (Thames & Hudson, 1957)

Johannes Bronsted, *The Vikings* (Penguin, 1960)

William R. Chaney, *The Cult of Kingship in Anglo-Saxon England* (Manchester University Press, 1976)

R. Elliott, *Runes* (Manchester University Press, 1963)

H.R. Ellis Davidson, *Gods and Myths of Northern Europe* (Penguin Books, 1964)

P.V. Glob, *The Bog People* (Faber & Faber, 1969)

P.V. Glob, *The Mound People* (Faber & Faber, 1974)

Manley Palmer Hall, *The Secret Teachings of All Ages* (Philosophical Research, 1962)

J.M. Kemble, *Anglo-Saxon Runes* (Andrew Publishing Co., 1976)

Margaret Murray, *The Divine King in England* (Faber & Faber, 1954); and an article, 'A Male Witch and his Familiar' in *Folklore* 1962

M. Osborn and S. Langland, *Rune Games* (Routledge & Kegan Paul, 1982)

Nigel Pennick, *The Swastika* (Fenris Wolf Publications, 1979)

Jurgen Spanuth, *Atlantis of the North* (Sidgewick & Jackson, 1979)

Tacitus *The Agricola and the Germania* (Penguin Books, 1948)

Richard Thonger, *A Calendar of German Customs* (Oswald Wolff, 1966)

Index